a Passion
for
Punchneedle

Edited by Linda Repasky

Martingale®
& COMPANY

A Passion for Punchneedle

Edited by Linda Repasky

© 2006 by Linda Repasky

That Patchwork Place® is an imprint
of Martingale & Company®.

Martingale & Company
20205 144th Ave. NE
Woodinville, WA 98072-8478 USA
www.martingale-pub.com

Printed in China
11 10 09 08 07   8 7 6 5 4 3 2

Mission Statement

Dedicated to providing quality products and service to inspire creativity.

Credits

President: Nancy J. Martin

CEO: Daniel J. Martin

COO: Tom Wierzbicki

Publisher: Jane Hamada

Editorial Director: Mary V. Green

Managing Editor: Tina Cook

Technical Editor: Carol A. Thelen

Copy Editor: Sheila Chapman Ryan

Design Director: Stan Green

Illustrator: Laurel Strand

Cover and Text Designer: Regina Girard

Photographer: Brent Kane

**Library of Congress
Cataloging-in-Publication Data**

Library of Congress Control Number:
2006020287

ISBN-13: 978-1-56477-711-9
ISBN-10: 1-56477-711-1

Contents

Getting Started

You are about to enter the enticing and addictive world of miniature punchneedle embroidery. And what a wonderful world it is—handwork that is not only quick and easy, but also creates the most charming and lush results. Miniature punchneedle offers you that exquisite blend of engaging handwork and meditative rhythm, and you won't exhaust yourself with following minutely detailed instructions and charts.

Why have so many people fallen in love with punchneedle work? Here's what I hear most often.

- Punching creates beautiful pieces that are so rich they beg to be touched.

- With only one stitch to learn, you can master it within minutes.

- It provides instant gratification. You can finish a project in a matter of a few hours.

- It allows you to use a plethora of threads and fibers that you may already have on hand.

- It's portable—tuck it into a small bag and take it with you to soccer games or waiting rooms.

- It's soothing and has a gentle rhythm—perfect for picking up at the end of a busy day.

- It has few rules, so the sky's the limit in what you can do with it.

- It's just plain fun!

So let's get started with the basics of how to punch. For more detailed instructions, check your library or bookstore for my first book, *Miniature Punchneedle Embroidery: Simple Techniques, Beautiful Projects* (Martingale & Company, 2006).

The Basic Supplies

Following is a list of the basic supplies you'll need. Note that good, strong lighting is also necessary and is much more important than having any kind of magnification. A gooseneck desk lamp is a good choice, or any lamp that allows you to adjust the direction of light.

Punchneedle. Miniature punchneedles come in a variety of sizes and forms with plastic or metal handles. One of the key differences between types of punchneedles is in how they allow you to adjust the length of your loops. Some punchneedles have a spring mechanism to move the needle; these use the end of the handle to create a barrier to stop the needle. Other punchneedles adjust loop length by adding or removing short lengths of plastic tubing (gauge) that are cut to size and slipped over the needle. The projects in this book use one-strand, three-strand, and/or six-strand punchneedles.

A few of the many punchneedles available: Igolochkoy, Bernadine's, CTR, Super Luxo, and Cameo Ultra Punch

Embroidery hoop. Punchneedle requires working on exceptionally taut fabric, so you will need an embroidery hoop or frame that is capable of gripping the fabric tightly. Avoid wooden hoops that allow the fabric to slip. Look for a plastic hoop with an interlocking lip. Another option is to use a gripper frame made specifically for miniature punchneedle. The gripper frame grips and holds the fabric so firmly that it doesn't require tightening and adjustment.

An embroidery hoop with an interlocking lip or a gripper frame holds the fabric taut.

Tightly woven fabric. Punchneedle work generally requires tightly woven fabric. The best fabric for this is weaver's cloth, a cotton/polyester blend. The polyester adds resiliency, allowing you to punch and repunch areas without worrying about the fabric ripping. Look for weaver's cloth on bolts at most fabric stores. Other woven fabrics, such as muslin, can be used, although there's a risk that they could tear. You can also punch on loosely woven fabrics, or even on nonwoven fabrics such as knits and sweatshirts, as long as you apply a fusible woven interfacing to hold the loops in place.

Threads for punching. You have many thread options. Most people use six-strand cotton embroidery floss. This floss comes in many colors, and can be separated into six strands. Hand-dyed cotton embroidery floss offers variation in colors and values within a single skein. Pearl cotton and cotton sewing-machine thread are also great for punching. Wool threads are beautiful for punching, too, since they give your work a softer, matte appearance. You can also punch with silk threads to get silk's unique sheen. Virtually any fiber that flows through the needle can be used, so don't hesitate to experiment!

Scissors. You'll need a pair of small, sharp scissors with thin blades for clipping threads very close to the backing fabric. My favorite scissors to use when punching are Havel's Snip-Eze.

Weaver's cloth, floss, threads, and embroidery scissors

Preparing Your Fabric and Thread

Cut an 8" square of fabric. Separate the rings of your embroidery hoop and place the inner ring on a table with its lip facing up. Look for the raised lettering on your hoop that says "This side up"—this is a critical step! Place the fabric on top of this. Open up the outer ring as far as you can and slip it on top of the fabric. Press down on the outer ring until it pushes down over the fabric and inner ring. Pick up the hoop and fabric and push the outer ring slightly below the inner ring, until you hear a click as the outer ring settles below the lip of the inner ring.

Tighten the screw of the outer ring until you sense that the fabric is beginning to tighten. Gently pull on the fabric, all the way around, and tighten the screw some more. Keep repeating this sequence, gradually tightening the fabric until it is very tight in the hoop. The fabric should be in the hoop on the straight of grain; try to keep the threads of the fabric at right angles as you tighten. Your fabric should be drum tight. When you think you've tightened the fabric as much as you can, go back and tighten it some more! Your hoop may begin to look more like an oval than a circle—that's okay.

If you have a gripper frame, set your fabric on top of the gripper strips. Use both hands to pull the fabric over the strips, first on the sides, and then on the top and bottom. "Walk" your hands all the way around the frame to tighten the fabric until you're satisfied with how taut it is. You are aiming for fabric that is drum tight.

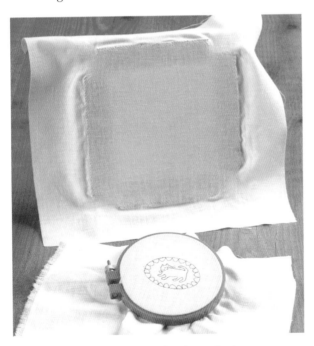

The fabric stretched tight in the hoop and the gripper frame

If you're using six-strand cotton embroidery floss, you'll need to separate the strands before punching. Cut a 36" length of floss from the skein. Gently tap the newly-cut end so that the strands begin to loosen and grab one of the strands. While holding that single strand with one hand, hold all six strands tightly with your other hand using your thumb and forefinger. Now pull the single strand away from the others.

The floss will scrunch up in your palm as you pull, but will relax as soon as the single strand is removed. Repeat to pull out additional strands one at a time as needed.

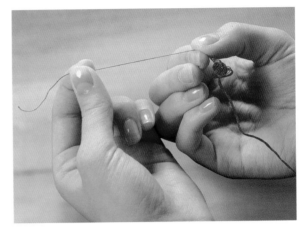

Separating six-strand cotton embroidery floss

Threading the Punchneedle

After preparing your fabric, you're ready to thread your punchneedle. Here are the steps for using a threader for a short-handled punchneedle (longer handles require a longer threader, and a slightly different process; refer to the instruction sheet that came with your punchneedle to see how it's done).

1. Notice that one end of the threader has a loop and the other end is blunt. Insert the looped end into the hollow tip of the punchneedle. Push the threader through the needle and through the handle until the loop pokes out of the top by about an inch or so.

Insert the threader from the tip of the needle until it pokes out the top of the handle.

2. Insert the required number of strands of floss into the looped end. Insert only a few inches of floss—just enough for the threader to grip. Give the floss a gentle tug toward the loop to keep it firmly in place as you continue threading.

3. Grab the other end of the threader and pull the entire threader, along with about 6" or 7" of floss, out of the tip of the needle. Don't remove the floss just yet.

Once the floss has been inserted into the loop, pull the threader toward the tip until several inches of floss have emerged.

4. Push the blunt end of the threader into the eye of the needle and pull it all the way through, along with several inches of floss.

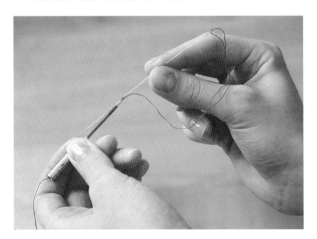

Threading is complete! The floss is through the eye of the needle.

5. Remove the floss from the threader. Then place your threader in a safe place, such as onto a magnetic strip adhered to the inside lid of your sewing box.

6. Gently pull back on the floss coming out of the handle so there's about an inch of floss poking out of the eye.

Ready to punch—you'll need only about an inch of floss extending from the eye of the needle.

How to Punch

It's important to know which way the needle is facing when you're punching. The needletip is beveled on one side and this beveled edge is the *front*. The side with the eye is the *back*.

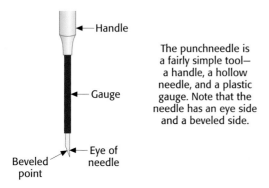

The punchneedle is a fairly simple tool—a handle, a hollow needle, and a plastic gauge. Note that the needle has an eye side and a beveled side.

Punch from right to left if you're right-handed and from left to right if you're left-handed.

- If you're right-handed, the bevel faces left, and the eye, with a tail of floss hanging from it, faces right.

- If you're left-handed, start punching at the left end of a row and move toward the right. The bevel of the needle will be facing right, and the eye of the needle, with a tail of floss, will be facing left.

Some punchneedles have a line marked on the handle to indicate the bevel side of the needle. If yours doesn't have a mark, you can easily add one by painting a dot or line using brightly colored fingernail polish. Many people find this helpful to ensure that their needle is facing the correct direction.

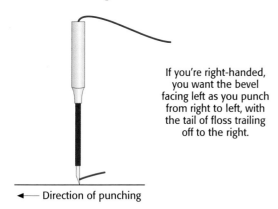

If you're right-handed, you want the bevel facing left as you punch from right to left, with the tail of floss trailing off to the right.

Since you will be working from the back, you will not see the loops forming on the front as you punch. You'll want to flip your work over often to see how things are shaping up on the front side.

Okay, let's start punching!

1. Hold the punchneedle at a 90° angle to the fabric in the hoop.

2. Insert the tip of the needle down into the fabric as far as the needle will go. It can go only so far, because the gauge (or the end of the handle) will stop it.

3. When your needle can go no further, lift it up gently. The tip of the needle should come just barely above the surface of the fabric. Take care not to lift too high or you'll risk pulling out the loop you just made.

4. With your needle tip at the surface of the fabric, drag the punchneedle over a distance of perhaps a thread or two to the left if you're right-handed (or to the right if you're left-handed). The needle tip should be scraping the fabric. Now push the needle down into the fabric again as far as it will go to make another loop, and then lift up to just barely above the surface of the fabric.

5. You're punching! Continue to make this basic stitch over and over to create a lush row of loops.

Every time you push the punchneedle down into the fabric and lift up again, you are creating a little loop. When you drag the needle over to create the next stitch, you are moving just a tiny amount. By spacing the loops closely together, the loops will be dense and none of the backing fabric will peek through on the front. Practice punching straight and curvy lines. Punch a square to practice turning corners. Punch another square outside the one you just punched, using a different color of floss, to get a sense of what happens when you punch two different colors side by side.

Punchneedle creates a surface that is so dense you don't need to use knots or glue to hold the loops in place. Make sure you carefully clip any loose threads on the back of your work since these could result in pulled loops. Every time you begin punching with a new piece of thread, you'll have a short piece of thread sticking up from the fabric (this is the tail that ran from the eye of the needle when you made your first loop). After you've made several loops, stop and clip off the thread as close as possible to the surface of the backing fabric. This will ensure that the loops stay snugly in place. Keep punching until you run out of thread.

When you reach the end of an area using one color and you still have thread in your punchneedle, it's easy to change to another color. Place your finger on the thread where it comes out of the fabric and press down with your fingernail to hold the thread in place. Use your other hand to lift up the punchneedle 1" or 2". Use your scissors to clip the thread as close to the fabric as you can. Rethread your punchneedle with the new color.

When you finish with one color of thread, clip the thread as close as possible to the fabric. Rethread with a new color and resume punching.

Helpful Hints

Here are some handy hints to keep in mind as you punch.

Keep the flow of thread loose! As you punch, take care not to let anything obstruct the flow of thread through the handle and needle. If the flow is obstructed, you'll end up with very short loops or no loops at all. It's easy to lean your arm or hand on the thread without realizing it. To help prevent this, run the thread up along the top of your arm to keep it out of harm's way.

Punching around curves and corners. When you're punching around a curve or corner, don't turn your punchneedle. Instead, keep your punchneedle stable and turn your hoop. This is far easier to do and creates a more even punched line.

Outlining as you punch. Unless the pattern instructions state otherwise, always begin by punching one row to outline each motif or design element. This will ensure that you have a nice crisp edge. Use the same color as you'll use in that section of your pattern. Your pieces will look even better if you outline each color again, this time with the adjacent color. For example, if you're punching a yellow star against a black background, first punch one row of yellow to outline the star. Next, fill in the star with more yellow. Then punch a single row of black loops all the way around the star to outline it before you fill in the rest of the black background.

Direction of punching. When filling in a large motif or background, you might be tempted to punch in straight lines. There's no rule that says you can't do this, and in fact, there might be times when you want the effect of straight lines running across your piece. It's often more interesting, though, to punch in undulating curvy lines or in other irregular patterns. For example, when filling in a design element, simply continue to punch around and around the shape, echoing the shape until it's completely filled in. You can punch backgrounds by echoing the shapes in the foreground, or by punching spirals or swirls in backgrounds—this makes it more interesting to look at and to punch.

Fill in larger expanses of motifs and backgrounds by echoing the shapes that have already been punched. Continue echoing until no empty spaces are left.

Indistinct lines and shapes. Sometimes when you punch two different colors beside one another, you don't always get the crisp, distinct line you were expecting. Loops can become intermeshed as you're punching, resulting in loops of different colors mingling together when you want them to stand alone. You can fix these indistinct lines and areas by coaxing loops back to their proper place. Use the tip of your punchneedle or scissors to carefully groom your piece, loop by loop, to tuck stray loops back into place. Although this process can try your patience, it's worth the effort, since it can make a big difference in how your piece looks.

Stray threads and long loops on the top of your piece. You may sometimes have stray threads appear on the front of your work (the loopy side). This happens as you run out of thread—the end of your thread has nowhere to go, and just sticks up above the level of the other loops. You might also occasionally have an extra-long loop on the front. This happens when you accidentally punch into an existing loop, pushing it out. Clip off the stray thread or loop to make it level with the other loops, or use a very fine crochet hook (0.75 mm) to pull the thread or loop to the back. Clipping the thread or loop can create a slightly darker appearance; if this bothers you, use the crochet hook instead.

Spacing of loops. You want the individual loops in a row to be very close together. However, when you're filling in an area and have several rows side by side, the spacing between rows needs to be a bit further apart. The general rule of thumb is to punch rows of loops about one needle-width apart. You *want* to have some white space on the *back* of your pieces—aim for having thin rows of fabric showing between rows of punching. If you punch the rows too close together, then your piece could be overpunched, resulting in a piece that curls and resists lying flat.

Individual loops should be punched
very close together, but rows
of punching should leave a small
amount of white space on the back.

Loop length. You can change the loop length quite easily by adjusting the gauge. With most plastic-handled needles, you can adjust the gauge on the handle by pressing a spring-loaded lever or by screwing the needle farther in or out. With most metal-handled punchneedles, you can add or remove the plastic tubing (gauge). To make your loops longer, slip the gauge off the needle and use a razor blade to cut off a short piece of the gauge; then place the original piece back on the needle. To shorten your loops, find the extra gauge material that came with your punchneedle and cut off a short piece with a razor blade. Slip this little piece onto the needle next to the longer piece of gauge. Add or remove small pieces of gauge until you find the loop size you like best. The longer the gauge, the shorter the loop.

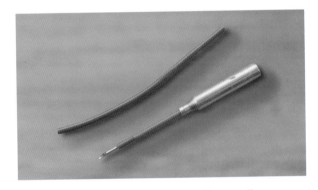

*The gauge, slipped onto the needle,
controls the length of loops.*

*Adjust loop length by slipping
small pieces of gauge onto your needle.*

The order of punching. The general rule is to begin punching in the center of the piece and move outward. If your design is a cat lying on a rug, punch the cat first. Begin by punching the eye, nose, whiskers, and any other internal lines (perhaps the line of a leg). Outline and then fill in the cat shape. Outline the rug, as well as everywhere the cat's body touches the rug; then fill in the rug. For the background, punch a single row to outline the cat and the rug; then punch a single row to outline the outer border. Finally, fill in the background.

The back of your piece. You want the back of your piece to look smooth and neat. At first, you might be lifting the needle a little too high, making small loops on the back. That's okay when you're starting—but work toward having a nice flat back to your piece. Loops on the back can easily be pulled out.

*Strive to create a flat, smooth
back with no stray threads.*

Starting a design. When you first begin punching, your work may not look as nice as you hoped it would. The loops may be flopping every which way, creating a disappointing blob. As you add more loops, you'll find that all the loops together will support one another and your motifs will begin taking shape. Don't feel disheartened and pull out your loops when you're first beginning a project—this messy stage is a natural part of nearly every piece.

Mistakes. If you've used the wrong color somewhere, or don't like the way your loops are looking, it's easy to pull them out and repunch the area. Weaver's cloth is very resilient and forgiving, so you should have no trouble repunching into the same area. Once you pull out the loops, scrape the surface of the fabric with your fingernail to help the weave return to place.

Transferring Designs to Fabric

Before beginning any project, you'll need to transfer the pattern onto your backing fabric. Here are three methods.

Drawing Directly on the Fabric

Draw directly on the fabric using a fine-point permanent marker. I use the Pigma Micron pen, which is archival and does not bleed when used on fabric. If your design includes any letters or numbers (or anything else where direction is critical), draw these in reverse so when you punch them from the back they will have the correct orientation on the front.

Using an Iron-On Transfer Pen or Pencil

Draw the pattern onto tracing paper or other lightweight paper using an iron-on transfer pen or pencil (these can be found in the notions department of fabric stores). Place the drawing, face down, onto the backing fabric. Following the directions that came with your pen or pencil, use a hot iron to transfer the design onto the fabric. This process automatically reverses your design, so when you punch letters or numbers, they'll turn out just fine.

Using a Light Box

Draw the pattern onto tracing paper or other lightweight paper. Place the paper onto the light box; then place the fabric on top of the paper. The light box produces enough light to let you see the design clearly through the fabric, so all you need to do is trace the design with a permanent fine-point marker. Reverse any design that has letters or numbers. If you don't have a light box, you can improvise. Tape your design to a window on a sunny day and trace onto fabric that way. Alternatively, place a lamp on the floor between two chairs under a piece of glass that rests on the chairs; then place your drawing and fabric onto the glass.

Here's one more pointer—virtually every fabric has some stretch to it. As a result, the finished piece may be slightly larger than the actual pattern you're using. If your punched piece requires a precise size or shape, transfer your design onto the fabric *after* you've stretched it in your hoop or frame.

Finishing Your Piece— What's Next?

In this chapter, we'll cover the basics of how to finish your piece, and explore different ways of displaying your work. You can frame your punched pieces, or add them to other items. For example, you can easily cut an opening into the lid of a small papier-mâché box and insert your punched piece. Or, transform an ordinary photo album into something special by attaching a punched design onto the front cover. Stay alert to the potential use of objects we see every day. The photo below may give you some additional ideas.

- A metal basket or "pocket" with a handle—glue a punched piece to the front
- A Christmas ornament with a photo insert—slip a punched piece inside
- Wooden box—attach your punched piece to the lid
- Scrapbooking frame—frame a punched piece
- Basket—attach a punched piece to one side
- Notebook cover—stitch a fabric cover and attach a punched piece

This photo shows a variety of objects that would look great with an applied punched piece.

First Things First—When You Finish Punching

Here's a checklist of the things you'll want to do with every piece when punching is complete.

1. Check the front carefully before removing it from the hoop. Are there any bare spots where you can see the backing fabric from the front side of the piece? If so, you'll want to fill in those sections with more loops. To help you find the precise spot where you want to add loops, poke a straight pin through the fabric wherever loops are sparse; then flip over your piece and punch in the area of the straight pin.

   You'll also want to clip off any stray threads or loops that are higher than the rest of the finished surface, or use a tiny crochet hook (0.75 mm size) to pull the strays to the back.

   Are there any motifs that have scraggly outlines or edges? Using the tip of your punchneedle or sharp scissors, move the stray loops back to where they belong.

2. Check the back for loose threads before removing the finished piece from the hoop. Clip the threads as close to the back of your piece as possible.

3. Remove the piece from the hoop. It should lie fairly flat. If it's puckering or cupping, it's likely that you punched your loops too close together. You can likely fix this in the next two steps (and in the future, try to punch your loops a little further apart).

4. Steam your piece. Place your punched piece face up on a soft towel on your ironing board. Use steam and the wool or cotton setting of the iron. Hold the iron about an inch above the loops for several seconds so the steam can penetrate the fabric. Allow the piece to dry before moving it.

5. Press your piece. If your piece is curling or cupping, then you'll need to add another step. Lay your piece, loops facing down, on a soft towel on your ironing board. Dampen a pressing cloth and lay it over your piece. With the iron set on cotton or wool, gently press your piece by setting the iron in one spot and holding it in place for several seconds. Flip the piece over, redampen the pressing cloth, and press again from the front, this time exerting very little pressure. Allow the piece to dry.

   A note of caution: some hand-dyed flosses and threads may not be colorfast—their colors could bleed with moisture and heat. Watch your piece carefully as you steam and press.

Preparing Your Finished Piece

You will need to trim and finish the edges around the completed piece so the backing fabric will not fray. Two of the methods described below use glue, and two use thread. Many people consider using glue to be quickest and easiest, while others avoid using glue to avoid potential problems with glue chemicals that might cause fibers to break down over time. Choose the method that's best for you. If you decide to use glue, take care not to let any of it seep through to the front of your loops.

The Glue Method

This method is great for curvy or irregular borders. Place your finished piece, front side down, on a square of wax paper. Apply a thin bead of fabric glue along the fabric just beyond the last row of loops. Use your finger to gently spread the glue along the entire perimeter, as well as about ¼" into the backs of the loops. Dry thoroughly. Use scissors to cut as close as you can to the last row of punching, without cutting into any of the loops. You will be cutting *through* the dried glue. Cut with the loops facing up so that you can avoid cutting into them. The dried glue will prevent fraying.

Apply a thin layer of glue on the back,
just beyond the last row of punching,
and about ¼" into your loops.

The Fold-and-Glue Method

This method works best with straight borders. Trim the fabric ½" away from the outer loops. Fold this fabric to the back, trying to get the fold as close as you can to the last row of loops. Fold the corners first; then fold the sides over the corners to form a miter at each corner. Finger-press a crease in each fold. Open the fold and apply a thin bead of glue to the underside of the fabric. Glue and press down on the corners, and then glue and press down on the sides. Allow the piece to dry.

The Archival Method

Trim the fabric to about ½" from the outer loops. Fold this ½" of fabric to the back—first the corners, and then the sides to form a miter at each corner. With sewing thread and needle, stitch the sides together at each corner to hold the miter in place. And you're done!

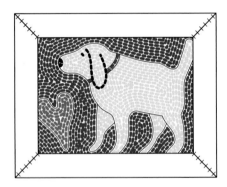

Stitch a few stitches back and forth
across the sides of the miter.

Whipstitched Edges

In addition to finishing the edges of your punched piece, whipstitching creates a decorative border. Simply trim back any excess fabric to about ½" from the last row of loops. Thread and knot a #18 chenille needle with floss or thread in a matching or coordinating color. Use six strands of cotton embroidery floss, or three strands of wool thread. Fold the excess backing fabric toward the back, leaving about 1/16" of fabric showing on the front.

Begin at a point near a corner. Insert the needle into the backing fabric inside the fold to hide the knot. Bring the needle through the fabric on the back and

bring it forward toward the front. Insert the needle down into the fabric right at the edge of the outside row of loops and pull the thread through. Now bring the needle up and around, from the back to the front, and make another stitch very close to the previous one. Continue making these simple stitches very close together to create a dense surface that conceals the backing fabric. Periodically stop to flatten the threads and check for good coverage over the fabric. When you reach a corner, make multiple stitches in the same spot to completely cover the fabric. Complete the entire outside border. When you reach the starting point, insert the needle into the fabric and aim toward the fold. Knot the thread, and you're done!

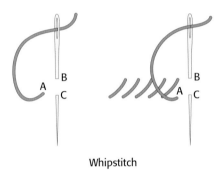

Whipstitch

Twisted-Cording Edges

Another alternative for adding a decorative edge is to use twisted cording. Once the backing fabric is protected from fraying by using any of the glue, fold-and-glue, or archival methods described above, twisted cording gives your punched piece added dimension and beauty. Your local fabric store *may* have the color and thickness you need, or you can create cording that is exactly what you want. Many of us made this kind of cording as kids by tying some yarn to a doorknob and using our hands to twist the fiber until it was tightly wound. This same method still works!

1. Choose two colors of floss that coordinate with the outside border of your punched piece. You can use all six strands of each cotton floss, or you can use more or fewer, depending on how thick you want your cording to be. Cut each piece of floss to about four times the length of the outside measurements of your piece (for example, a 2" square has a total length of 8"; multiply this by four to get 32").

2. Tie a knot at each end to create one big loop. Tie one end to a hook or drawer handle and pull back on the loop of floss. Slip the other end over your index finger.

3. Begin to move your index finger in circular motions, as if you were dialing a telephone. Keep "dialing" until the floss is tightly wound, making sure that you keep tension on the floss.

4. Once it's quite tight, use your free hand to press down on the midpoint of the twisted floss. While keeping the twisted floss pulled tight, bring the two loose ends together at the hook or handle.

5. Holding both loose ends of the floss together, let go of the center and watch the floss twist tightly onto itself. Tie a knot to hold the ends in place.

6. Thread a sewing needle with a single strand of floss (one of the colors used for the cording). Use this to stitch the twisted cord around the edges of your piece. Make simple overcast stitches about ¼" apart.

For more detailed instructions and illustrations on twisted-cording edges, see pages 29–30 in *Miniature Punchneedle Embroidery*. You can also use a tool like the Spinster to create twisted cord. More information can be found on my Web site (www.woolenwhimsies.com).

Framing Your Piece

One of the most common ways to display punched pieces is to frame them. I like to use fabric as a mat. Cotton quilting fabric is available in countless colors and prints; textured cottons, wools, silks, and other fabrics are equally effective display options. Here are the fundamental steps involved in preparing a piece for framing.

1. Finish the edges of your punched piece using your choice of finishing methods described in "Preparing Your Finished Piece" (page 15).

2. Apply twisted cording (page 16) if desired.

3. Cut a piece of archival acid-free mat board slightly smaller than the frame opening (to allow for the thickness of fabric covering the edges of the mat board).

4. Cut the fabric several inches larger than the mat board.

5. Center your punched piece on the fabric and sew it down using an invisible hand stitch. Smaller pieces need only a few stitches at each corner. Larger pieces may need to be stitched all the way around.

6. Center the fabric on the mat board and fold the edges to the back.

7. Working from the back, use heavy-duty thread to lace the fabric closed. Stitch from top to bottom, pulling each stitch very tight, then stitch from side to side. Flip the piece over periodically to check that your punching is still centered.

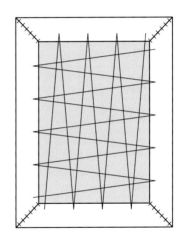

Fasten your piece onto mat board, sewing from top to bottom and side to side.

8. Slip the fabric-covered mat board into the frame and enjoy!

Making a Wearable Pin

Pins make lovely gifts, are quick to punch, and show off your pieces to their best advantage. Several pin projects are included in this book. Here are the basic steps for creating a pin.

The supplies you'll need:

- 1¼" pinback

- A small piece of plastic, cardboard, or other stiff, flexible material (I like to use heavyweight quilter's template plastic.)

- Sewing thread and needle

- A piece of felt or wool in a color that matches the outside border of your piece

1. Finish the edges using either the glue method (page 15), the fold-and-glue method (page 16), or the archival method (page 16).

2. Cut a piece of plastic or cardboard ¾" smaller than the outside border of your punched piece (for example, for a 2" square piece, cut the plastic or cardboard to 1¼" square).

3. Using a small amount of fabric glue, center and glue the plastic or cardboard piece to the back of your punched piece. Allow to dry.

4. To back the pin, cut a small piece of wool or felt at least as big as the outside dimensions of your piece. Position the pinback on the wool or felt slightly higher than center and sew in place.

5. Glue the piece of wool or felt (with pinback attached) to the plastic or cardboard (with punched piece attached). Dry thoroughly.

6. Trim the wool or felt to the size of your punched piece. I trim mine to about ¹/₃₂" beyond the edge of my punched piece. This creates a tiny ledge for the twisted cording or whipstitched edge.

7. Whipstitch (page 16) or attach twisted cording (page 16) to finish the edges.

Creating a Necklace Pendant

Another great way to wear your pieces is to make them into pendants. Depending on the type of hardware you use, pendants can be even quicker than making pins. See the Kitty Pendant (page 22) for an example.

You'll need a firm base of some kind. I prefer to slip my punching into a tiny (1" wide and 1½" high) pendant frame. Check the jewelry, scrapbooking, or beadwork sections of your craft store to find small frames used as charms and page decorations.

The specifics of making a pendant will depend on what kind of base you'll be using. Here are instructions for using the small flip-top frame shown in the photograph below.

The tiny frame has a hinged top,
making it easy to insert your punched work.

The supplies you'll need:

- Small pendant or charm frame

- Small pieces of mat board

- Small piece of wool, felt, or other fabric

- Fabric glue

- Sewing needle and thread (optional)

1. Measure the opening of the frame and cut two pieces of mat board slightly smaller than the outside dimensions of the frame (to allow for the thickness of fabric covering the edges of the mat board).

2. Trim the backing fabric to about ½" beyond the last row of punched loops.

3. Center your punched piece on one of the mat board pieces. Starting with the corners and then the sides, fold the backing fabric to the back. Keep your eye on the front to make sure the design stays centered.

4. Use glue or lacing (see "Framing Your Piece" on page 17) to attach the punched piece to the mat board. If using glue, place a book on the pieces to help the glue adhere as it dries.

5. For the exposed back of the frame, cut a piece of felt, wool, or other coordinating fabric to the size of the frame. Use fabric glue to attach this fabric to the second piece of mat board. Allow to dry.

6. To complete the framing, slip the mat board with your punched piece into the frame, with your punching facing outwards. Insert the backing mat board with the felt or wool facing outward.

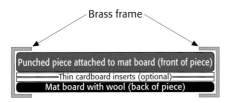

Bird's-eye top-down view.
Cardboard and mat-board pieces
hold the punching firmly in place.

7. Your punching should be firmly in place within the frame. If it seems loose, cut a piece of thin cardboard or poster board to the size of the frame and slip it between the two pieces of mat board. Keep adding thin pieces until the punched piece feels solid.

8. Click the top of the frame closed and attach a length of ribbon, rattail, or cording through the top. Your beautiful new piece of jewelry is ready to wear and enjoy.

*A finished punched piece
fits perfectly inside the frame.*

Embellishing Books

Imagine embellishing the cover of your favorite journal, sketchbook, photo album, scrapbook, or calendar with your beautiful handwork. In many cases, you can simply attach your punched piece directly to the cover. Finish the piece with whipstitching or twisted cording, and then use an adhesive that is compatible with both the fabric and book. Many adhesives labeled "tacky glue" work very well for this purpose.

Embellishing Boxes and Other Containers

You can apply a punchneedle piece to virtually any kind of box and container. Look around the house to see whether you already have any boxes, tins, or jars that could be improved with the addition of a punched piece. Many boxes you can use "as is," while others may need painting, covering, or cleaning. Several projects in this book explain how to apply punched pieces to boxes and other containers. For step-by-step instructions for one beautiful method for covering boxes, see Raspberry Clusters Box (page 53).

Embellishing Clothing

To embellish a piece of clothing with a punched piece, you can punch directly onto the clothing as long as the fabric is fairly tightly woven. If the clothing has a loose weave or is a knit, you can still punch into it by applying a fusible woven interfacing to the back. Draw your design onto the interfacing before fusing it to the clothing. Punch through both layers, adjusting the gauge to account for the additional thickness. You will most likely need to punch longer loops. When the clothing is washed, the fibers will tighten, which will help hold the loops in place. No need for special washing methods! Remember, though, that some threads might not be colorfast when washed.

If there's not enough room for a hoop, punch a design onto a separate piece of fabric and then appliqué the finished piece onto the clothing. Finish the piece by sewing it on with an appliqué stitch, or use flexible, washable fabric glue.

Quick Ways of Finishing Punched Pieces

Some punched pieces deserve fancy presentation. But others may be perfectly suited for fast finishing methods. Here are a few to consider:

Bottle caps. Draw a design (on fabric already stretched in a hoop) to fit inside an unused bottle cap. Finish the edges using the glue method described earlier in this chapter. Use glue to adhere the punched piece to the bottle cap and allow to dry. Use as a magnet by applying a piece of adhesive magnetic tape to the back. Or, make the bottle cap into a pin by using metal glue to attach a pinback. Bottle caps can be found in the scrapbooking sections of craft stores, and in beer- and winemaking supply stores.

Decorative magnet. Recycle business card advertising magnets. Use glue to attach your finished punched piece to the magnet. If your piece is smaller than the magnet, use scissors to trim the magnet to the desired size.

Coin purse. Stitch a finished punched piece onto the side of a small change purse found at department or discount stores. Fabric or woven-straw purses are ideal for this.

Bookmark. Punch a long, thin design onto fabric. Finish the edges and stitch onto a slightly larger piece of wool or cotton fabric (to create a thin border around your piece).

Coaster. Punch a design that will fit onto an existing round or square coaster. Use glue to apply. Or, attach your punched piece to an appropriately sized piece of cork or felt to create a coaster in a custom shape and size.

Photo box or photo album. Many of these boxes and albums are available with a square or rectangular cut-out area on their covers. Simply insert a punched piece into the opening, and voilà, instant finishing!

The Projects—A Feast
for the Eyes and Spirit

Hang on to your hat—you're about to see an amazing array of beautiful punched projects. Thumb through the following pages and see how punching can take everyday objects to new heights of beauty and creativity. The projects are presented in order of difficulty, from beginner to advanced. Make the projects precisely as they're presented, or use them as a launch-pad for your own creations.

Suggestions for loop length are offered for each project. To measure the gauge (for example, if the instructions say the gauge is set at ⅜"), focus on the portion of the needle that's exposed between the eye of the needle and the end of the gauge (or the end of the handle). That exposed portion of the needle should be equal to the measurement noted in the project instructions.

A note on the project directions you'll be reading: you'll see that there are some inconsistencies in approach and instructions as you move from one project to the next. Each of the designers has found her own method of punching, just as you will.

Enjoy your explorations of the rich and enchanting miniature punched pieces on the following pages!

Kitty Pendant

by Linda Repasky

Skill Level: Beginner • **Finished Size of Punching:** 1" x 1½"

This is the perfect beginner's project!
The small brass frame is a wonderful complement
for this charming kitty. You'll be amazed
at how quickly you can finish an entire project.

What You'll Need

3-strand punchneedle

Embroidery hoop or gripper frame

8" square of weaver's cloth

Small brass pendant frame, 1" x 1½"
(see "Resources" on page 74)

2" x 2" piece of black wool

Several small pieces
of mat board or cardboard

Waxed linen thread for whiskers

Black satin rattail cording

Fabric glue

Wool Threads

One skein of each. Use either DMC Medicis for solid colors or Needle Necessities French Wool Overdyed for gentle fluctuations in color—or mix and match. The project in the photo was punched using French Wool Overdyed.

Used For	Color	Medicis		French Wool Overdyed
Head, body	Creamy tan	8502	*or*	21
Facial features, collar	Brown	8611	*or*	25
Background	Dark red	8100	*or*	53

Punching

The pattern appears on page 66. Use one strand of thread in the three-strand punchneedle. Pieces this small generally look better with a shorter loop length, so set the gauge to ¼".

1. Using the brown thread, create the collar by punching two rows, side by side, along the collar line. Punch two or three loops very close together for each eye; then punch the nose using one row of loops.

2. With the creamy tan thread, punch a single row of loops all the way around the head, around each eye, and then around the nose. Outlining the facial features gives shape to the face. Fill in the rest of the head, face, and body with the creamy tan thread.

3. Using the dark red thread, punch a single row of loops to outline all portions of the cat that touch the background. Punch a single row of loops along the outside border of the piece. Fill in the background. Punch in echoes around the cat; or punch random squiggles and then fill in around them. Doing this gives your piece subtle movement, which is more interesting to look at than straight rows.

Finishing

1. Steam the punched piece and let dry.

2. Thread a sewing needle with a 12–18" length of waxed linen thread (found in the beading section of craft stores). Create whiskers by taking single stitches into the punched piece. Insert the needle from front to back on one side of the nose, move the needle along the back, and insert it on the other side of the nose, pushing the needle up through the punching from the back. Pull on the needle to leave 1" of thread exposed on the side of the nose where you first inserted the needle. Clip off the thread, leaving another 1" on the other side of the nose. Repeat twice more.

3. Follow the instructions in "Creating a Necklace Pendant" (page 18) for inserting your kitty into a pendant frame.

Potted Pin

by Shawn Williams

Skill Level: Beginner • **Finished Size of Punching:** 2½" diameter

Who doesn't love pins? This punchneedle pin
on a 2½" cover button makes a fabulous one.
The cover button keeps it strong and
durable, and finishing is fast and easy.

What You'll Need

3-strand punchneedle

Embroidery hoop or gripper frame

8" square of wheat- or khaki-colored weaver's cloth

Dritz Company 2½"-diameter half-ball cover button

Metal pinback and glue

Cotton Embroidery Floss *One skein of each.*		
Used For	**Color**	**Weeks Dye Works**
Border	Purple	Mulberry
Background	Black	Onyx
Flower pot	Brick red	Chrysanthemum
Flower stem, leaves	Green	Kudzu
Flower petals	Gold	Whiskey
Flower checkered center (light)	Beige	Beige
Flower checkered center (dark)	Brown	Chestnut

Punching

The pattern appears on page 66. Use two strands of floss and a ⅜" gauge.

1. When transferring your design onto fabric, align the design so the stretch of the fabric is parallel to the arrow drawn on the pattern. Transfer the dotted outer line, which will be your cutting guide when the punching is complete.

2. Use purple floss to punch two rows of loops for the outer border.

3. Punch the rest of the piece in the order of the floss listed in the chart above; outline each motif before filling it in.

Finishing

1. Trim the punched piece on the dotted outer line.

2. Place the piece over the cover button. The cover button made by the Dritz Company is particularly easy to use because it has outer teeth that help you adjust your punched piece into place. Work from top to bottom and side to side until you have the piece centered in place and secured on the teeth.

3. Remove the wire bar inside the cover button.

4. Snap the back cover in place.

5. Glue the pinback on and you're finished!

Memory Gift Jar

by Margaret Shaw

Skill Level: Beginner • **Finished Size of Punching:** 2½" diameter

Margaret loves to use found materials in her folk-art work.
For this simple project, she used a canning-jar lid as the frame and
template to draw the original circle. A ribbon or gift tag may be
added to decorate your jar. It is best to add dry contents only.

What You'll Need

3-strand punchneedle

Embroidery hoop or gripper frame

11" square of weaver's cloth

5" length of double-sided ⅝" fusible tape

4" x 4" square of lightweight
fusible interfacing

Small-mouth (2½") canning jar
with lid and ring

Cotton Embroidery Floss One skein of each.		
Used For	**Color**	**The Gentle Art**
Leaves, stem	Green	Dried Thyme
Star points	Black	Black Crow
Circle behind star	Red	Mulberry
Outline of red circle	Burgundy	Cherry Bark
Flower center outer circle	Gold	Grecian Gold
Flower center inner circle	Off-white	Shaker White
Background	Tan	Flax

Punching

The pattern appears on page 66. Use three strands of floss and a ⅜" gauge.

1. Before transferring your design to the fabric, draw a 2¾" circle. To do this, use the 2½" jar lid as a guide and draw a circle about ⅛" away from the edge. This circle is the outside border of your punched piece—if you punch to the circle, you'll have complete loop coverage inside the opening of the jar lid.

2. Transfer the design onto the fabric, centering it in the circle. Outline each motif and fill it in using the photograph as a guide to color placement. As you punch, keep the following tips in mind.

   • Make sure the star points extend beyond the circle behind them.

   • As an option for the stem and leaves, you could use several shades of green to simulate a hand-dyed look.

   • For gentle highlights, you may choose to outline the star, circle, and leaves with a lighter tan or cream.

Finishing

1. Lay your punched piece face down on a soft towel and gently press. Trim the fabric ¾" away from the outer border of the punched piece.

2. Using the lid as a template, cut a circle of fusible interfacing and follow the manufacturer's instructions to fuse it onto the back of your punched piece.

3. Use a small pair of scissors to clip about ½" into the fabric all the way around the circle, about every ¾". Take care to avoid clipping into any punched areas. Fold the fabric to the back and use double-sided fusible tape to fuse it down onto itself.

4. Place the punched piece into the ring, centering the design. Place the lid over the back and screw it onto the jar.

Baby Block Tote Bag

by Charlotte Dudney

Skill Level: Beginner • **Finished Size of Punching:** 2¼" x 2¼"
Finished Size of Bag: 5" x 5"

You can decorate any ready-made denim
or canvas bag with punchneedle. This cute bag
will make a great gift for any new mother.
Just think of the possibilities!

What You'll Need

3-strand punchneedle

Embroidery hoop or gripper frame

8" x 8" square of weaver's cloth

5" x 5" x 2" natural-colored canvas tote

2¼" x 2¼" square of lightweight woven fusible interfacing

Cotton Embroidery Floss

One skein of each. Use either the Finca by Presencia or the DMC—or mix and match. The project in the photo was punched using Finca by Presencia.

Used For	Color	Finca		DMC
Background of each block	Pale yellow	7128	*or*	746
B, border of Y block	Purple	2615	*or*	553
A, border of B block	Pink	1729	*or*	603
B, border of A block	Blue	3312	*or*	3325
Y, border of B block	Green	4388	*or*	563

Punching

The pattern appears on page 67. Use three strands of floss and a ⅜" gauge.

1. Turn the tote inside out and transfer the pattern onto the wrong side of the bag.

2. With pale yellow, punch the background of each block. Punch right beside the lines of the pattern rather than punching on top of the lines. This will leave you enough room to punch the letters.

3. Use pink to punch the letter *A*. Punch inside the lines. Use blue to punch around the outside of the block.

4. Use purple to punch the letter *B* on the top row of blocks. Use green to punch around the outside of the block.

5. Use green to punch the letter *Y*. Use purple to punch around the outside of the block.

6. Use blue to punch the remaining letter *B*. Use pink to punch around the outside of the block.

Finishing

1. Remove the tote bag from the hoop and carefully iron it to remove the crease created by the hoop. Slide the edge of the iron around the outside of the design to lift up the outside row of punched loops.

2. Use fusible interfacing to protect the design from being snagged while the tote bag is in use. To do this, place a washcloth inside the bag (which is still turned inside out) to protect the punched surface. Following the manufacturer's instructions, fuse the interfacing to the back of the punching. If your bag has nylon handles, be careful not to iron them—they could melt.

3. Turn the tote bag right side out and fill it with shampoo, powder, teething rings, pacifiers, or toys—the perfect gift for a new mother!

Winterberry Keepsake Tin

by Cherie Ralston

Skill Level: Beginner • **Finished Size of Punching:** 3" diameter

This charming tin is the perfect pin box to use in your sewing basket,
or perhaps to safely hold jewelry at your bedside. The folk-art design
was inspired by an antique quilt and is punched with both
solid and hand-dyed floss to give the piece an aged look.

What You'll Need

3-strand punchneedle

Embroidery hoop or gripper frame

10" square of weaver's cloth

3" round Altoids or mint tin

Rubber cement

Barn red spray paint

Wide rubber band

½" x 11" strip of wool fabric

1 small brown button

3" circle of blue wool or felt

10" x 10" square of cotton batting

Cotton Embroidery Floss One skein of each unless otherwise noted.			
Used For	**Color**	**DMC**	**The Gentle Art**
Tree trunk, lower branches	Brown	433	
Leaves, upper branches	Green	731	
Berries	Red	3777	
Star, outer background	Blue		Brethren Blue (2 skeins)
Inner background	Cream		Buttercrunch (2 skeins)

Punching

The pattern appears on page 67. Use three strands of floss and a ⅜" gauge.

1. Transfer the tree and star motif onto the fabric; then stretch it in your hoop or frame and transfer the circle, the wavy border, and the dots.

2. Punch the motifs in the order they appear in the chart above using the colors indicated. For each motif you will outline first; then fill in.

3. For the inner background, use the Buttercrunch floss to punch a single row of loops along the wavy border.

4. With Buttercrunch, outline a single row of loops around the trunk, each leaf, each berry, and the star. Fill in the interior background and punch the eleven small dots that float in the blue background.

5. With blue floss, work the outer background by punching a single row of loops along the outside border (a 3" circle). Punch a single row of loops along the wavy border of Buttercrunch and a single row of loops to outline each of the eleven small dots. Fill in the outer background.

Finishing

1. Remove the punched piece from your hoop or frame and steam it. Trim the fabric to 1½" from the last row of loops. Hand sew a running stitch ¼" from the trimmed edge. This running stitch will be used later to gather the piece around the lid. Set aside.

Sew a running stitch
¼" from the trimmed edge.

2. Next, prepare the tin. With the lid off, place the tin upside down on newspaper and spray paint the bottom and sides only. Allow it to dry thoroughly. On the side of the lid stamped "Press to open," make a mark with an indelible marker. This mark is used later to line up the bottom of the tree.

3. Use the lid as a template to cut four circles of cotton batting. Cut two circles the same size as the lid and two circles slightly smaller. Stack the batting circles on top of each other, with the two largest at the bottom.

4. Spread rubber cement on the outer side of the lid and set it aside to dry. On the back of the punched piece, brush a ring of rubber cement about 1/2" wide along the edge of the punching. The dried rubber cement acts as a gripper later to help the two surfaces stick together. You do not need to spread rubber cement on the back of the loops; keep the adhesive on the backing fabric only. Let dry.

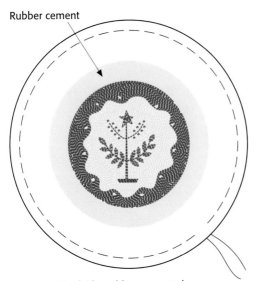

Rubber cement

Apply the rubber cement along
the edge of the backing fabric
(but not on the outer row of loops).

5. Place the stack of batting circles on top of the lid and place the punched piece on top of them, lining up the tree base with the mark on the side of the lid. Pull the threads of the running stitches to gather the circle around the lid. Line up the edge of the punching with the edge of the lid. Press the glued edges of the punched piece to the glued edge of the tin. Secure with the wide rubber band and allow to set.

6. Remove the rubber band. Trim the edge of the fabric even with the edge of the lid. Use the wool strip to cover the fabric on the side of the lid. Place one end of the strip on the side of the lid at the base of the punched tree. Use a small dot of rubber cement to hold the end in place, and then pull the strip firmly around to cover the fabric, adding dots of rubber cement as you go to hold the strip firmly in place. Overlap the ends by 1/2". Sew or glue the button on the overlapped ends.

7. Use the base of the tin to trace a circle onto the 3" piece of wool or felt. Cut this fabric slightly smaller than the circle so it will fit snugly inside the tin. Use rubber cement to adhere the circle to the inside bottom of the tin.

8. Fill the tin with your treasures and enjoy!

Two Rabbits Needle Case

by Karen Amadio Gates

Skill Level: Intermediate • **Finished Size of Punching:** 3½" x 2½"
Finished Size of Needle Case: 4" x 3"

The inspiration for this project was a rug made by Maria Warning,
an artist from Perth County, Ontario, who made several rugs in the
late nineteenth century. Maria's style is distinctive; she often
used a diagonal hit-or-miss border, hearts in the corners, and
a horizontal hit-or-miss background. Karen used artistic license
and punched each rabbit in a slightly different color for added interest.

What You'll Need

1-strand punchneedle

Embroidery hoop or gripper frame

8" x 8" square of weaver's cloth

4" x 6" piece of green felted wool

3½" x 5¼" piece of rose felted wool

#18 chenille embroidery needle

3¼" x 2¼" piece of shirt cardboard

Sharp embroidery scissors

Pinking shears

Liquid seam sealant

Optional: ⅜" or ¼" black snap closure

Cotton Embroidery Floss *One skein of each.*					
Used For	**Color**	**DMC**	**The Gentle Art**	**Weeks Dye Works**	**Needle Necessities**
Rabbit	Deep tan		Woodsmoke		
Eyes, lettering, background	Black			Onyx or Charcoal	
Heart outlines, stitching the needle-case pages	Dusty rose		Old Brick		
Rabbit, heart centers	Tan		Fudge Ripple		
Heart inner borders, lettering outline	Dark mustard	167			
Border	Dark blue, rose, and tan				127
Buttonhole stitching	Green floss to match your green wool				

Punching

The pattern appears on page 68. Use one strand of floss and a $^3/_{16}$" gauge.

1. Transfer the design to fabric. You may elect to punch your initials or another significant date beneath the rabbits. Transfer whatever numbers or letters you wish to use backward so that they will come out the right way in the finished work.

2. Punch the eyes using Onyx. They will be football shaped, with four or five closely placed stitches.

3. One rabbit is punched with Fudge Ripple and the other is punched with Woodsmoke. Outline the bodies; then the eyes. Finally, fill in all the inner parts.

4. With Old Brick, punch two rows to outline each of the four hearts. With Dark Mustard, punch one row along the inner edge of the Old Brick. Use Fudge Ripple to fill in each heart center.

5. Punch the lettering using Onyx; then punch around the outside of the lettering using Dark Mustard.

6. Punch the background with Onyx. Outline each shape and the inner rectangle; then fill in the centers. Punch the outer rectangle on the *out-side* of the line. The diagonal hit-or-miss border is punched within this remaining area.

7. The hit-or-miss border is the fun part if you have the right thread! The Needle Necessities 127 (overdyed in shades of dark blue, rose, and tan) gives the appearance of a hit-or-miss style when you punch in diagonal lines. If you are unable to find this thread, use several colors of floss from your stash to create a similar look by punching one diagonal row of each color to create the hit-or-miss pattern.

Finishing

1. After removing the piece from the embroidery hoop, let it rest a bit to relax the fabric. Carefully iron up to the edges of the punching. Trim the excess fabric to ½". Apply a liquid seam sealant or fabric glue along the outer rows of loops, on the back side, to ensure the loops stay in place. Allow the adhesive to dry.

2. Follow the instructions in "Whipstitched Edges" (page 16) to whipstitch the edges of your punched piece. You'll also insert a piece of shirt cardboard to add firmness to your finished piece. To do this, first whipstitch along a short side; then a long side; and then the other short side. Slip the piece of cardboard under the back side of your punching, tucking it underneath the three small folds of excess backing fabric on the sides that you've already whipstitched. Whipstitch the remaining long side of the piece. This will encase the cardboard behind your punching. Set aside.

3. Using a green cotton embroidery floss that blends into the wool color, sew a row of buttonhole stitches all the way around the outside edge of the green wool.

4. Fold the green wool in half from top to bottom. Center the punched piece on the front of the wool and use the matching floss to hand sew it to the wool. Hide the thread inside the thickness of the wool as you sew and space the stitches about ¼" apart. Stitch to the ditch that is created between the very last row you punched and the whipstitched edge.

5. Trim the piece of rose wool to 3¼" x 5" with pinking shears. Fold it in half and place it inside the green wool, matching the fold lines. Using two strands of Old Brick floss or a rose-colored sewing thread, hand sew the two folds together along the fold with a row of running stitches, hiding the knots inside the green wool.

6. If you like, add a snap to the inside. Slip some needles into the rose-colored pages and enjoy.

A Rose for Mommy Clock

by Tonya Benson

Skill Level: Intermediate • **Finished Size of Punching:** 6" diameter
Finished Size of Clock: 9½" x 11½" x 2½"

After making a hooked-rug clock face, it seemed only natural for Tonya to apply the same technique to punchneedle. Tonya likes to create mottled backgrounds by using two or more similar colors of floss. She alternates different colors of short lengths of floss, about 24", to create the delightful random mottled appearance that is typical of many primitive hooked rugs. The project name came out of the mouths of babes when her five-year-old child said that the design was "a rose for Mommy."

What You'll Need

3-strand punchneedle

Embroidery hoop or gripper frame

11" x 11" square of weaver's cloth

Clock frame with 6"-diameter opening

Clockworks

Fabric glue

Cotton Embroidery Floss *One skein of each unless otherwise noted.*		
Used For	**Color**	**DMC**
Leaves	Green	3013, 3052
Leaf veins	Dark green	936
Center of flower	Dark shell grey	451
Rim of center flower and petal highlights	Dusty rose	3773 (2 skeins)
Petals without highlights	Rosewood	3858, 3859
Petals with highlights	Terra cotta	355, 356
Numerals	Desert sand	3064
Background	Dark khaki	3787, 844, 640 (2 skeins each)

Punching

The pattern appears on page 67. Use three strands of floss and a ⅜" gauge.

1. Leave the X at the center of the flower unpunched; this is where you'll later insert the arms of the clock. Outline, and then punch the center of the flower and the petals. Use the colors as shown in the chart above.

2. Punch the veins of the leaves with dark green. Outline the leaves and each vein with green (#3052). Fill in the interior portions of the leaves using the other green (#3013).

3. Punch the numerals of the clock face with one row of loops.

4. Punch the background, alternating the three background colors. You can punch small sections of colors, or you can punch in echo lines around the motifs—the background can be as random as you like to create a primitive feel.

Finishing

1. Paint or stain the clock in any manner you choose. A slightly distressed finish complements the primitive look of the design.

2. Following the manufacturer's instructions, mount the clock's shaft in the wooden clock case.

3. Remove the punched piece from the hoop and trim the excess fabric to 1½" to 2" beyond border.

4. Turn under the edge of the fabric and glue it to the back of the punched piece.

5. Using a pencil, poke through the X at the center of the punched piece. Center it on the clock shaft, placing the numbers in the correct position.

6. Lift the edge of the punched piece and apply glue. Press the punched piece against the clock frame until it lies flat.

7. Refer to the manufacturer's instructions to finish placing the clock hands.

Bird Blue Pillow

by Pat Cross

Skill Level: Intermediate • **Finished Size of Punching:** 6¾" x 4½" • **Finished Size of Pillow:** 16" x 12"

Pat's home state of Virginia is a haven for English bluebirds. Bird Blue Pillow
is her primitive interpretation of these wonderful creatures, which nest
in many of the birdhouses in her yard. The background of this piece is
left unpunched, leaving the fabric exposed, and reverse punching
is used in some places to create flat stitches.

What You'll Need

3-strand punchneedle

Embroidery hoop or gripper frame

9" x 11" piece of khaki weaver's cloth

16" x 12" pillow form

20" x 36" piece of blue plaid fabric

12" x 18" piece of red plaid fabric

Cotton Embroidery Floss *One skein of each.*			
Used For	**Color**	**Weeks Dye Works**	**The Gentle Art**
Bird, berries, head and tail feathers	Teal	Twilight	
Bird, berries, head and tail feathers	Teal	Chesapeake	
Bird	Teal	Brethren Blue	
Eye, stripes, feet, daisy and tulip centers, berries, head and tail feathers	Dark tan	Cocoa	
Feet	Greenish brown	Swamp Water	
Daisy and tulip centers, berries	Light brick		Gingersnap
Daisy and tulip petals, berries	Brick		
Daisy and tulip petals, berries	Rust	Rust	
Daisy and tulip petals	Burgundy	Indian Summer	
Vines	Green		Blue Spruce

Punching

The pattern appears on page 68. Use three strands of floss, except as noted below, and a ⅜" gauge.

1. Using two strands of Cocoa, punch the bird's eye.

2. To punch the body, you'll use a few different blends of floss in your needle, combining specific colors. To outline the bird, punch two rows, alternating the following blends.
   - Two strands of Twilight and one strand of Chesapeake
   - Two strands of Brethren Blue and one strand of Chesapeake
   - Two strands of Brethren Blue and one strand of Twilight
   - One strand each of Twilight, Chesapeake, and Brethren Blue

3. Punch the vertical stripes on the body using a blend of one strand each of Twilight, Chesapeake, and Cocoa. Fill in the rest of the body with three strands of floss, using your preferred blend of Chesapeake, Twilight, and Brethren Blue.

4. Punch the feet (two or three rows of loops) using two strands of Swamp Water and one strand of Cocoa.

5. For the daisy, punch the inside circle using two strands of Gingersnap and one strand of Cocoa. Outline and fill in each petal using one strand each of Brick, Rust, and Indian Summer.

6. For the tulip, outline each of the three petals with two strands of Gingersnap and one strand of Cocoa by punching two or three rows of loops. Fill in each of the petals using one strand each of Brick, Rust, and Indian Summer.

7. The berries are punched using two strands of floss in various color blends. Punch several berries with each blend. Pat used the following blends.
   - One strand each of Brick and Rust
   - One strand each of Twilight and Chesapeake
   - Two strands of Gingersnap
   - One strand each of Brick and Cocoa

8. For a change in texture, flip your piece over and punch from the *front* side to create flat stitches in these sections.
   - Vines: three strands of Blue Spruce
   - Head and tail feathers: one strand each of Twilight, Cocoa, and Chesapeake

Finishing

Use a ½" seam allowance to construct the pillow. All measurements include seam allowances. Steam press around the punched design to remove any creases left by your hoop.

1. With the punched design centered, trim the piece to measure 9½" x 7".

2. From the red and blue plaid fabrics, cut the pieces shown in the chart below.

Piece	Red Plaid	Blue Plaid
A (cut 2 pieces)	4" x 7"	
B (cut 2 pieces)	3½" x 15½"	
C (cut 2 pieces)		2" x 12"
D (cut 2 pieces)		2" x 17½"
Pillow backing (cut 1 piece)		8" x 17½"
Pillow backing (cut 1 piece)		11" x 17½"

3. For each of the two pillow backing pieces, fold and stitch a ½" hem along one of the 17½" sides.

4. Using the diagram as your guide, stitch the remaining red and blue plaid pieces to the punched piece in the order listed below, always stitching with right sides together, and then pressing in the direction of the piece being added.

- One red plaid A to each side

- One red plaid B to the top and one to the bottom

- One blue plaid C to each side

- One blue plaid D to the top and one to the bottom

5. With right sides together, sew the smaller backing piece to the top of the pillow. Match the raw edges and sew around the three sides. Sew the larger backing piece to the bottom of the pillow, again matching the raw edges. The backing pieces will overlap each other, leaving the hemmed edges open to insert the pillow form.

6. Turn inside out and insert your pillow form through the opening in the back.

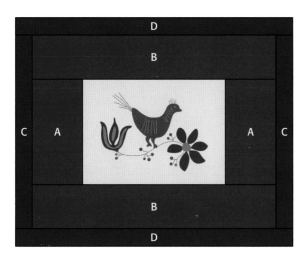

Snowman's Candy Jar

by Brenda Gervais

Skill Level: Intermediate • **Finished Size of Punching:** 3¾" x 3¾"

During the Christmas holidays, Brenda transforms her home into a winter wonderland that's filled with her collection of vintage Christmas villages, snowmen, and Santas. This punchneedle design fits in perfectly! Brenda displays the snowman on a reproduction pantry jar—just like the one she remembers her grandmother storing her sugar in.

What You'll Need

3-strand punchneedle

Embroidery hoop or gripper frame

11" x 11" square of weaver's cloth

8" x 6" glass pantry jar

Red gloss spray paint

Spray adhesive or fabric glue

Coarse sandpaper

Craft glue

Peppermint candies

Cotton Embroidery Floss *One skein of each unless otherwise noted.*		
Used For	**Color**	**DMC**
Eyes, mouth, coal buttons, hat, inner border	Black	310
Stripe on hat	Red	347
Carrot nose	Burnt orange	301
Twig arms	Tan	642
Narrow stripes on scarf	Sky blue	825
Wide stripes on scarf	Green	988
Snowman, ground, snowflakes	Off-white	Ecru (2 skeins)
Sky	Blue	598 (2 skeins)
Candy cane border	Red	Used above
Candy cane border	Off-white	Used above
Outer border	Black	Used above

Punching

The pattern appears on page 68. Use three strands of floss and a ³⁄₈" gauge.

1. With black floss, punch the eyes, mouth, buttons, and a single row of loops for the inner border.

2. Punch each part of the snowman and background in the order listed in the floss color chart. First outline, and then fill in.

3. Punch the narrow red stripes of the candy cane border using two rows of loops. Rather than punching right on the line, punch one row slightly to the left and one row slightly to the right of the drawn line.

4. Punch the outer border using three rows of black loops.

Finishing

1. Trim the excess fabric ½" from last row of loops. Fold the excess to the back and finger-press a crease along the last row of loops.

2. Unfold the fabric and cut away a small square at each corner to reduce bulk. Use spray adhesive or fabric glue to adhere the folded fabric to the back of the punched piece.

3. For a better bond between the punched piece and the glass, use coarse sandpaper to sand the area of the glass to be glued.

4. Apply craft glue to the back of the punched piece. Glue the punched piece securely to the jar. Allow to dry.

5. Spray the lid with one or two coats of red gloss paint and allow to dry. Fill the jar with peppermint candies and enjoy!

Beach Crab Basket Topper

by Linda Stolz

Skill Level: Intermediate • **Finished Size of Punching:** 4¼" x 3½" • **Size of Basket Lid:** 6" x 4"

Punch this fun little crab with its quirky grin to add
to your beach collectibles. This design is embellished
with seashells and made into a topper for a charming
Nantucket basket. The project is fun and colorful, and
incorporates a bit of metallic thread in the water for some shimmer.

What You'll Need

1- and 3-strand punchneedles

Embroidery hoop or gripper frame

10" x 10" square of khaki weaver's cloth

Rainbow Gallery Treasure Braid Petite
#PB62, Morning Waters

Nantucket style basket,
approximately 6" x 4½"

2 size 8 black beads from
Mill Hill #18014 (optional, for eyes)

Fabric glue

Mat board or firm cardboard

Piece of thin cotton batting
(slightly larger than basket opening)

Piece of coordinating cotton fabric
(slightly larger than basket opening)

Sewing needle and strong sewing thread

30 small seashells,
approximately ½" to ¾" wide

Cotton Embroidery Floss				
One skein of each. Where two colors are given, blend the colors, or use only one.				
Used For	**Color**	**Weeks Dye Works**	**The Gentle Art**	**DMC**
Sand	Light tan	Fawn		
Water	Blue	Blue Topaz		
	Aqua	Caribbean		
Wave crest	White and light blue	Icicle		
Sky	Light blue	Morris Blue	Pomegranate	
Crab	Deep rose			
Mouth, eyes	Black	Mascara		
Twisted cord				612 and 613

Linda suggests that you work your way down from the largest areas toward the little details, because otherwise the small areas might get buried. She prefers to wait and leave the details for last to make them "pop." She also recommends that you don't punch on the actual lines of the pattern; punching on the lines could cause too much intermingling of the threads wherever two colors comes together.

Punching

The pattern appears on page 69. Use one strand or three strands of floss, as specified in the instructions below, and a ⅜" gauge on both sizes of punchneedles. Use the one-strand punchneedle when using one strand of floss and the three-strand punchneedle when using three strands of floss.

1. Using three strands of Fawn, punch the sand along the bottom.

2. Using one strand of floss, punch the water. Alternate three colors of thread to get a multicolored and shimmering look as follows. Starting around the outside, punch a few rows of Blue Topaz, followed by a few rows of Caribbean, and then a single row of Treasure Braid Petite. Keep repeating this pattern until the water is filled in. Make thread combinations as random or regular as you like—it's a great opportunity to "paint" with these colors!

3. Use Icicle to create the crest of the wave.

4. Use Morris Blue to fill in the sky.

5. With Pomegranate, fill in all the areas of the crab, leaving only a bit of space for the mouth and eyes.

6. With one strand of Mascara, fill in the mouth with a few rows of punching. Make a few punches for the eyes, or use shiny black beads instead.

7. Before removing the piece from the hoop, you might also want to clip a few of the sand loops here and there to add to the texture of the beach.

Finishing

1. Remove the piece from your hoop; press lightly.

2. Using the basket as a guide, trace an oval that is slightly larger than the top of the basket onto a piece of paper. Use this template to cut a piece of mat board or firm cardboard for the topper (making the topper larger than the basket opening prevents it from falling inside). Cut one or two layers of thin cotton batting a bit larger than the topper—enough to roll over the edge, but not wrap to the back side. Glue the batting to one side of the topper and let dry.

3. Using a needle threaded with strong sewing thread, make running stitches in the fabric all the way around your punched design, placing the stitching about 1" beyond the outer row of loops so that the sewing thread won't show on the upper side of the topper.

4. Center the punched piece on the topper; pull the running stitches to gather the fabric so the design is snug and centered on the topper. Tie a square knot in the thread to secure it. If you need to smooth out the gathered edges a bit more, make another row of running stitches on the bottom within ¼" of the topper edge. When you tighten up this last row of running stitches, knot the thread to secure it.

5. Trim out any excess bulk created by the gathered fabric and secure the fabric edges with glue as needed. You want a fairly flat surface on the bottom of the topper. Set it aside for now.

6. Cut another piece of mat board smaller than the first—this one will fit *inside* the basket to prevent the topper from slipping off the basket. Cover with one layer of batting for a softer look. Using a coordinating fabric, cover this piece just as you did with the top layer. After trimming the bulk from this inside piece, glue it to the bottom of the topper, hiding all raw edges between the layers. Anchor the two halves together so they don't slip while the glue dries by putting them under heavy books or other weight. If the inside piece doesn't cover the running stitches, remove the thread when the glue has dried.

7. With the DMC 612 and 613, make twisted cording long enough to span the outside edge of the topper. See "Twisted-Cording Edges" (page 16) for instructions.

8. Apply the twisted cording with the fabric glue. To cover any little imperfections, tuck the cording into the "ditch" created between the two layers of fabric on the lid.

9. Create another length of twisted cording and glue it to the edge of the punched design.

10. Finally, glue a row of seashells around the perimeter of the punched area.

Laura's Amaryllis Pillow

by Lee Faulkner

Skill Level: Intermediate • **Finished Size of Punching:** 6" x 4¼" • **Size of Pillow:** 20" x 11"

Lee's sister, Laura, recently purchased a gorgeous fabric for her kitchen curtains: black linen with colorful flowers and melons. Lee used this fabric as a jumping-off point for this design! This pattern has elements that extend beyond its border, but if you prefer, you can easily pull the pink flower back inside the border when transferring the design. The finished piece has been applied to a black cloth "apron" that ties with ribbons around a striped pillow.

What You'll Need

3-strand punchneedle

Embroidery hoop or gripper frame

14" x 14" square of weaver's cloth

½ yard of striped fabric for pillow
(cut into 2 pieces, 12½" x 21½" each)

2 yards of ⅜" purchased cording for pillow

2 yards of narrow ribbon for apron ties
(cut into 6 pieces, 12" each)

1 yard of black fabric for apron
(cut into 2 pieces, 14¼" x 24¼" each)

1⅓ yards of fringe for apron
(cut into 2 pieces, 24" each)

1 skein of DMC white #5 pearl cotton
for twisted cording for apron

1 skein of DMC black #5 pearl cotton
for twisted cording for apron

18 ounces of polyester fiberfill
or purchased pillow form

Cotton Embroidery Floss One skein of each unless otherwise noted.				
Pattern Key	**Color**	**DMC**	**Weeks Dye Works**	**The Gentle Art**
	Black	310 (2 skeins)		
1	Dark teal		Pea Coat (5 skeins)	
2	Red		Aztec Red (3 skeins)	
3	Creamy yellow		Honeysuckle	
4	Light rose		Cherub	
5	Green		Pistachio	
6	Green		Lucky	
7	Off-white			Oatmeal
8	Gold			Gold Leaf
9	Mustard yellow			Summer Meadow
10	Dusty rose			Old Brick
11	Green			Green Pasture
12	Blue			Blue Jay

Punching

The pattern appears on page 69. Use two strands of floss, except where noted below, and a ⅜" gauge. Refer to the pattern and the corresponding numbers on the chart (page 48) to determine which colors of floss to use as you punch.

1. Punch one row of black inside the wavy line of the border. Punch one row of black around all of the design elements to outline them. Leave enough room to punch the flower stems directly on the drawn lines.

2. Punch all of the flower stems directly on the lines using three strands of floss. Use Pistachio to punch the left stem, Lucky for the center, and Green Pasture for the right.

3. Outline and fill the larger design elements, carefully working around the smaller elements such as flower centers. Fill in the remaining small elements. Use Gold Leaf for the curved lines on the leaves of the center flower.

4. Fill in the background. Punch circles, swirls, and other shapes.

5. Using Aztec Red, punch one row along the outer rectangle; then punch one row next to the wavy black line. Fill in the border.

Finishing

1. Begin by making the pillow. With right sides together, pin the purchased cording to the outer edges of one of the pieces of striped fabric (this will become the pillow front). Machine baste in place. With right sides together, pin the two pieces of striped fabric together. Stitch using a ¼" seam allowance and leaving an opening along the lower edge large enough for turning and stuffing. Trim off the corners. Turn the pillow right side out and press. Stuff the pillow firmly. Slip-stitch the opening closed.

2. Next, make the apron onto which you'll attach your punched design. With right sides together, pin the fringe to both ends of one of the pieces of black fabric (this will become the apron front). Machine baste in place. (If the trim is exceptionally fluffy, you may wish to hand stitch the trim to the outside of the apron *after* construction.) Machine baste three ribbons on both ends of the apron front (one on each side and one in the center). With right sides together, pin the two pieces of black fabric together. Stitch, leaving an opening along one side large enough for turning. Trim off the corners. Turn the apron right side out and press. Slip-stitch the opening closed.

3. Tie the apron around the pillow before marking the placement of the finished punched piece. Turn under the edges of your punched piece, pin it to the apron, and slip-stitch in place.

4. Make twisted cording using the two colors of pearl cotton; see "Twisted-Cording Edges" (page 16). Stitch the twisted cording around the edges of your punched piece and enjoy your new pillow.

Stitcher's Dream Pouch

by Missy Stevens

Skill Level: Advanced • **Finished Size of Punching:** 2¼" x 2¼" • **Finished Size of Pouch:** 2¼" x 3"

Missy's design represents the four points on a compass and the continual movement of the wheel of life. Put tiny tokens that signify your hopes, dreams, and prayers into the pouch: words on paper, pebbles, charms, and so on. Missy used the smallest size punchneedle, threaded with two strands of *sewing thread*, for this project. Rather than punching loops close together, she widely spaced them, leaving large openings. She then went back to fill in the spaces with additional values and hues of color, giving her piece richness and depth. Missy cautions that, when wearing this pouch, you should avoid wearing jewelry that might snag the loops and pull them out.

What You'll Need

1-strand punchneedle

Embroidery hoop or gripper frame

8" x 8" square of off-white, tightly woven, high-quality quilter's cotton

Mother-of-pearl buttons:
¼" to ⅜" diameter—11
½" diameter—1
⅝" diameter—1

Size 11/0 cream seed beads (one package)

4" x 8" piece of off-white fabric for the flap and back. (Note: if you use fabric that frays, you'll also need 12" of ¼"-wide ribbon and seam sealant.)

1 yard of cord, ribbon, or braid for the neck strap

Beading needle

Iron-on transfer pen or pencil

Sewing Thread		
Choose two different shades of each color. Note that these are ordinary sewing threads. You will need one or two spools of each color as noted below. You may already have the perfect colors in your sewing box at home.		
Color	Shade #1	Shade #2
Yellow	2 different spools of light yellow	1 spool of rich yellow and 1 spool of gold
Orange	2 different spools of soft orange	1 spool of red orange and 1 spool of brick red
Green	2 different spools of light yellowish green	2 different spools of medium mossy green
Blue	2 different spools of light blue	2 different spools of medium blue

Punching

The pattern appears on page 70. Use two strands of thread and a ¼" gauge.

1. Transfer the pattern onto the backing fabric with an iron-on transfer pen or pencil. Be sure to include the letters indicating color placement.

2. Using your choice of thread, sew the 11 small buttons in place onto the front of your piece. For an elegant touch, you can use Buttonhole Twist silk thread. Follow the diagram for color placement. If your buttons don't fit in the circle, you may need to use fewer or more.

3. Sew the beads in place on the front. Use four seed beads for each bead "stitch."

4. Make sure that your punchneedle gauge is set so that the buttons and beads nestle nicely into the loops. (Missy used a gauge setting of ¼".) Begin punching the colors in the center of the button circle with the shade #1 colors. You will punch

with two threads simultaneously. Don't stitch too densely—punch just enough so that you start to see the colors. Place your individual loops about ⅛" to ¼" apart. Note that this is very different from the punching technique used for the other projects in this book! At this stage, punch sparsely, leaving lots of spaces that you can fill in later as the project progresses.

5. Stitch the areas between the buttons and the beads with the shade #2 colors. Stitch these areas densely because you won't be adding any shading.

6. Punch the area outside the beads with shade #1 colors, again not stitching too densely.

7. Go back into the center of the button circle and, using the shade #2 colors, punch more loops in the area punched in step 4 along the edges of the button only. Stitch the remaining center area densely with the shade #1 colors.

8. In the area outside the beads, punch three rows from the outside straight edges with the shade #2 colors, working through and between your existing loops. Then using the shade #1 colors, punch more loops in this area to make it lush and dense. Check the front of the piece to make sure there aren't any sparse areas, especially between the beads and the points between the buttons.

Finishing

1. When the loops on the front look nice and dense, remove your piece from the hoop. If the shape is distorted, block it by pinning it, wrong side up, onto your ironing board and then steaming it. Let the iron hover over it, but do not press the piece. Let it rest, pinned to the ironing board, for an hour to absorb its new shape.

2. Trim the fabric to ¾" from the last row of stitching.

3. Cut out the flap and back pieces for the pouch using the templates (page 70). If you are using fabric that is likely to unravel along the cut edges, use seam sealant to prevent that. Baste the flap to the punched piece, and then sew the two together using your machine. Have the embroidery on top so you can keep the stitches as close as possible to the punched loops. (It is helpful to use a zipper foot with the foot riding on the unembroidered fabric.) Press the seam flat.

4. Fold under the top edge of the back of the pouch twice. Each fold should be ⅛" to ¼" wide. This will make a nicely finished edge for the opening of the pouch. Press the folds, and then sew them using your machine.

5. Baste the back to the front, right sides together. Machine sew the pieces with the embroidery on top, stitching as close as possible to the outer rows of punching. Trim the seams to ¼". At this point you may need to retrim the point of the flap if it seems too wide or off center. (If necessary, use seam sealant again before cutting.) Turn the pouch right side out. Press gently with an iron.

6. Now you're ready to bind the raw edge of the flap with ribbon. First, press the ribbon in half lengthwise. Remember to turn the end neatly under as you start stitching (and when you finish). Hand stitch the long edge of the ribbon to the edge of the flap. When you reach the center point of the flap, stitch the edges of the ribbon together for 1" or 2" to create a button loop. Test your button to make sure the loop is the correct length. Then resume stitching the ribbon to the other length of the flap. When you've finished attaching the ribbon to the flap, press the edges you've just bound to make them crisp.

7. Attach the neck cord. If the cord might unravel at the cut edge, wrap it with thread. If you're using ribbon, turn the ends under. Stitch each end to the edges of the top of the bag, above the embroidery. Sew an ornamental button (⅝") on the center of the front, and the button for the flap (½") on the back.

Raspberry Clusters Box

by Patricia Smith Gardner

Skill Level: Advanced • Finished Size of Punching: 6" x 3½"

Patricia's inspiration for this piece was easy—she's a raspberry fanatic!
Patricia loves to create designs that are intricate, with lots of tiny detail.
This project is not for the puncher who wants to finish a piece in one day!
However, the finished product is one that you will
enjoy and appreciate for years to come.

What You'll Need

1-strand punchneedle

Embroidery hoop or gripper frame

10" x 10" square of ivory
or tan weaver's cloth

7½" x 5" x 3" papier-mâché
or cardboard oval box

Craft knife

Red acrylic paint

Black acrylic paint

Crackle medium

Satin clear acrylic spray

¼ yard of cotton batting

Fabric glue

Approximately 12 sewing pins

8" x 6" piece of heavy cardboard

Cotton Embroidery Floss One skein of each unless otherwise noted.			
Used For	**Color**	**DMC**	**The Gentle Art**
Background, checked border, outlining	Black	310 (2 skeins)	
Checked border	Ecru	Ecru	
Raspberries	Light red	347	
Raspberries	Medium red	498	
Raspberries	Dark red	815	
Leaves	Light olive	580	
Leaves	Dark olive	936	
Border	Deep red		Buckeye Scarlet
Stems, small leaves	Green and gold		Cornhusk

Punching

The pattern appears on page 71. Use one strand of floss and a ³⁄₁₆" to ¼" gauge.

1. To ensure the design retains the correct size and shape, transfer your design onto the fabric after you have tightened it on your hoop.

2. With black floss, punch the outline of the thin stems and small leaves at the base of the raspberries, and then fill in with the green-and-gold variegated floss. The variegated floss creates natural-looking shading.

3. With black, outline the raspberries; then fill in with the three colors of red as marked on the pattern: L for light red, M for medium red, and D for dark red.

4. Using black, outline the leaves and fill in the veins. Fill in the leaves with the two colors of olive as marked on the pattern: L for light olive and D for dark olive. The tips of the leaves should stick out into the border section a little.

5. Fill in all the background with black.

6. Punch the two rows of the red inner border. If you are using variegated red, do the rows side by side as a zigzag so that color changes in the thread stay together.

7. Punch the white squares of the checked border, and then the black squares.

8. Punch the two rows of the red outer border as you did the inner border.

Finishing

To finish this piece, you'll use a cardboard or papier-mâché oval box purchased from a craft store. Customize it by cutting an opening in the lid and mounting your punched piece.

1. To make the pattern for cutting out the center of the lid, draw the oval shape of your punched piece on paper and cut it out.

2. Center the pattern on the lid and draw around it with a pencil. Using a craft knife, carefully cut through the lid along the outline of the oval.

3. Apply a decorative finish to the box in four steps as described below. Allow to dry completely between coats.

   • With dark red acrylic, spray two coats on the lid and box, inside and outside.

   • Apply one coat of crackle medium to the outside of the lid and box.

   • With black acrylic, spray the lid and box, inside and outside. The black paint will crackle as it dries on the outside, allowing the red paint underneath to show through.

   • Spray a layer of clear satin acrylic on the lid and box, inside and outside, to seal it.

4. Trace the bottom of the box onto the cardboard and cut the cardboard along this shape. Place the cardboard inside the lid and trace the outline of the oval opening. Remove the cardboard. The smaller oval is where you'll mount your punched piece.

5. Cut three ovals from the batting. Cut the first to the size of the smaller oval on the piece of cardboard. Cut the second oval smaller than the first by ¼" all around. Cut the third oval smaller than the second by ¼" all around. These batting layers create a tapered padding for your punched piece.

6. Run a thin bead of glue all around the inside of the traced oval and center the largest batting piece on the oval. Center the second largest piece of batting on the first, and then center the smallest piece of batting on the second, using a few dots of glue to hold each layer of batting to the next.

7. Center your completed punched piece onto the padded cardboard with the back of your loops on the batting. Place the cardboard oval, with the punched piece on top of the batting, into the lid. Is the punched piece centered in the cutout oval? If not, gently adjust the fabric until it is centered. Once you're satisfied with the placement, pin your punched piece onto the batting to temporarily hold it in place and carefully remove the cardboard from the lid. Lifting the fabric edges of your punched piece a little at a time, glue it down around the cardboard border. Allow to dry. Trim away any excess fabric.

8. Glue the cardboard to the inside of the lid and allow to dry. You might want to glue an oval piece of fabric or decorative paper onto the inside of the lid so that the punched piece is protected. Or you can line the entire box and lid with fabric for a particularly luxurious feel.

October Bag

by Sally Korte and Alice Strebel

Skill Level: Advanced • **Finished Size of Punched Strip:** 11" x 2¼"
Finished Size of Punched Buttons: 1½" diameter

Sally and Alice love vintage textiles of all sorts, and have long collected
pieces that are interesting in texture, color, and technique. Here they punched
a whimsical strip of stars and candy corn to appliqué on a wool bag.
A delightful array of button covers gives you the option of making one
or a bunch to use on a bag or jacket of your choice.

What You'll Need

3-strand punchneedle

Embroidery hoop or gripper frame

½ yard of weaver's cloth

Handbag or tote bag, at least
11" wide (use a ready-made bag,
or make one from a pattern of your choice)

4 Dritz Company 1½"-diameter
#2 half-ball covered buttons
(optional—for the punched buttons)

Cording (optional—for the top
and bottom edges of the punched strip)

Cotton Embroidery Floss							
Floss amounts are provided separately for punching the strip of stars and candy corn and for the individual buttons.							
		Strip of Stars and Candy Corn	**Buttons**				
Color	**DMC**	**Skeins Needed**	**Skeins Needed**	**Jack-o'-Lantern**	**Candy Corn**	**Black Star**	**Gold Star**
Black	310	5	3	X	X	X	X
Gray	3021	3	1	X	X	X	
Red	349		1	X			
Gold	680	2	2	X	X	X	X
	320	2	2		X	X	X
Orange	920	5	3	X	X	X	
	3776	5	2	X	X		X
Cream	543	1	1		X		
	746	1					
Use three strands of floss and a ³⁄₈" gauge.							
Sally and Alice used solid-colored floss to create a mottled look. To do this, use several different shades of a color and, one at a time, fill in patches of colors until an entire section is filled in. By scattering values and colors, you'll create wonderful movement in your piece.							

Punching the Strip of Stars and Candy Corn

The pattern appears on page 72.

1. After transferring the design onto fabric, punch the stars, mixing areas of black and gray floss as described at the bottom of the chart (page 57). Punch the star background stripes by alternating the two shades of orange. Punch the triangles around the candy corn using the two golds.

2. Punch the tip of the candy corn with two colors of cream. Punch the next section with the darker orange, and the thin section with the lighter orange. Punch the bottom using the two golds.

3. Punch the background of the candy corn using black and gray.

4. Lightly steam press the piece, and then trim the fabric to ½".

Applying the Strip of Stars and Candy Corn

1. Fold back the excess fabric along the outer rows of punching, first diagonally across the corners, and then along the sides of the strip. Stitch the fabric at each corner to form a miter. This will hold the backing fabric in place.

2. Place the punched strip on the finished handbag or tote bag. Find a placement that pleases you and gently pin the strip in place.

3. Appliqué the punched strip to the bag. Stitch all the way around all four sides of the strip.

4. Attach a length of twisted cording along the edges, if desired.

Punching the Buttons

The patterns appear on page 72. Make one or make them all. Here are specific instructions for punching each button, followed by directions for assembling the buttons using purchased covered-button kits.

Jack-o'-Lantern Button

1. Punch the inner eyes (either with stars or circles), the pointed teeth, and the outline around the eyes and nose with black and gray floss. Punch the outline around the nose very tightly so it shows up well. Outline the eyes more sparsely so just a hint of outlining appears.

2. Punch the outer portions of the eyes using one of the gold colors.

3. Punch the nose with red.

4. Punch the background in stripes, alternating light and dark oranges.

Candy Corn Button

1. Punch the top of the corn using cream.

2. Punch the next section using dark orange, and then the thinner section using light orange.

3. Punch the bottom section using both golds.

4. Punch the background using black and gray.

Black Star Button

1. Punch the swirl in the center of the star using dark orange.

2. Punch the star with black and gray floss.

3. Punch the background using both golds.

Gold Star Button

1. Punch the star using both golds.

2. Punch the background by alternating rows of black and light orange.

Assembling the Buttons

1. Read the instructions on the package of buttons.

2. Trim the fabric to just under ½". Moisten the piece with a spray bottle or wet sponge. This helps mold the fabric around the button.

3. Center the design on the button and work the fabric over the edge of the button and onto the teeth. Keep moving around the button, catching the fabric tighter and tighter. The goal is to not see any of the fabric around the edge of the button.

4. Snap the back of the button in place.

Happy Jack Shoulder Purse

by Penny McAllister

Skill Level: Advanced • **Finished Size of Punching:** 4½" x 4¾" • **Finished Size of Purse:** 5½" x 6½"

An explosion of color, dimension, and texture is the hallmark of this practical shoulder purse. This piece is visually exciting because it uses bright primary colors in easy-to-find DMC embroidery floss, plus an assortment of beads and buttons, a punched bottle cap, and luscious black felted wool. Inspired by a papier-mâché piece by the same artist, this will surely become the most touchable piece of punchneedle embroidery you've ever created.

What You'll Need

1- and 3-strand punchneedles

Embroidery hoop or gripper frame

10" x 10" and 12" x 12" squares
of weaver's cloth

1 package of small,
multicolored rochaille beads

1 package of large,
multicolored rochaille beads

1 package of assorted alphabet beads

Assorted beads (bugle beads, miracle
beads, small glass beads) and buttons

1 package of small, black,
iridescent glass beads

Beading needle and threader

1 fat quarter of black felted wool

½ yard of medium-weight
fusible interfacing

1 fat quarter of fabric for lining

2 yards of ³⁄₁₆" black cording

Bottle cap (unused)

Small nail and hammer

Black sewing thread

Thin embroidery needle

Fabric glue

Cotton Embroidery Floss *One skein of each unless otherwise noted.*		
Used For	**Color**	**DMC**
Outlining, nose, border	Red	349 (2 skeins)
Eyes, teeth, dots	Ecru	Ecru
Block, details, eyes	Black	310
Pumpkin sections, block border	Dark orange	721
Pumpkin sections, block border	Light orange	741
Block border	Yellowish orange	742
Block border	Turquoise	958
Block border	Lime green	907
Hat, block border	Purple	552
Background	Magenta	718 (2 skeins)

Punching

The pattern appears on page 71. Use one, two, or three strands of floss as specified in the instructions below. The one-strand punchneedle is set to a gauge of ³⁄₈" to create short loops, and the three-strand punchneedle uses the gauge at varying settings, ranging from ³⁄₈" to ⁵⁄₈".

Pumpkin Piece

1. Transfer the pattern onto the 12" weaver's cloth and insert it into a hoop or frame.

2. Using one strand of floss, punch in the following order.

   • Red. Punch a single row of loops to outline the eyes, nose, mouth, teeth, pumpkin (including the section lines), stick, block, and hat. Fill in the nose.

- Red. Punch a single row of loops about one needle width away from the *inside* of the block border outline. Punch another single row of loops about one needle width on the *other side* of that same border outline, leaving a gap to accommodate a double row of loops that will be punched later. Punch the outside of the block border and then punch the horizontal lines that form the multicolored blocks.

- Ecru. Punch the outer and the inner sections of the eyes.

- White. Fill in the teeth and the dots on the block.

- Black. Punch three rows for each line on the hat. Punch the pupils with two rows of loops. Outline the white dots; then fill in the stick and the block. Fill in the six black border blocks as shown in the photo.

- Blue. Fill in the iris of the eyes.

- Dark orange. Fill in alternating sections on the pumpkin, beginning with the outer section.

- Light orange. Fill in the remaining pumpkin sections.

- Purple. Fill in the rest of the hat.

3. Switch to the three-strand punchneedle with the gauge set at $3/8$". Using one strand of light orange and one strand of black, fill in the pom-pom and the ruffles on the hat and neck.

4. Switch back to the one-strand punchneedle to fill in the multicolored border blocks as pictured. Note that the color order of the blocks is opposite from top to bottom and side to side. Fill in all the dark orange blocks, then the light orange, yellow, green, blue, and purple.

5. Fill in the background with two strands of magenta using the three-strand punchneedle with the gauge set at $3/8$".

6. Thread the three-strand needle with three strands of red with a $1/2$" gauge. Punch the gap between the magenta border and the block border with two rows of loops.

7. Still using three strands of red, punch three rows for the outer border using the three-strand punchneedle with the gauge set at $5/8$" for even longer loops.

8. Before you take your project out of the hoop, flip it over and check for any bare or sparse areas. Add more loops where needed. Check the front for any elongated or stray threads and clip where needed. Clip loose threads from the back. Spread a small bead of seam sealant around the outer edge of the punched piece and let it dry while the piece is still in the hoop.

Bottle Cap

1. Transfer the bottle-cap pattern onto the small piece of fabric. Remember that numbers are punched in reverse.

2. Insert the fabric into a hoop or frame. Using the one-strand punchneedle, punch the numbers with one strand of black floss. The bottle cap commemorates the jack-o'-lantern's special day—October 31!

3. Fill in the background with one strand of yellow floss. Check the front for bare areas and fill in with more loops where necessary. Clip loose or stray threads on the front and the back.

4. Before removing your fabric from the hoop, put a bead of seam sealant around the outer edge of the back side of the stitching. Make sure you get it on the first few rows of loops along the outer edge, as well as into about $1/4$" of the backing fabric. Set the piece aside to dry (in the hoop).

Embellishments

With the piece still in the hoop and working from the front, place and then sew each bead randomly as listed below using a beading needle and one strand of matching floss or sewing thread.

1. Scatter large black glass beads in the magenta background.

2. Scatter small orange and yellow rochaille beads on the face and small red rochaille beads on the nose. Add clear rochaille beads to the teeth and the innermost part of the eyes.

3. Sew the large clear rochaille beads on the dots on the block.

4. Scatter different sizes of the rochaille beads on the block border, matching up the colors of the beads with the blocks when possible.

5. Sew the alphabet beads, spelling *HAPPY JACK,* on the bottom row of the block border.

6. Scatter more of the rochaille beads on the bottom border.

7. String some of the small black beads and sew them onto each stripe of the hat.

8. Embellish the bottle-cap piece with a few of the yellow and orange rochaille beads.

9. Remove the pumpkin piece from the hoop and trim the backing fabric to ½". Fold the fabric back and whipstitch (see "Whipstitched Edges" on page 16). Remove the bottle-cap piece from the hoop and trim it as close to the stitching as possible. Set aside.

Finishing

1. Cut a piece of the wool, the interfacing, and the lining fabric to 6" x 14". Fold the lining piece lengthwise, right sides together. Sew a ⅝" seam down both 7" sides. Turn the lining piece inside out and press flat. Set aside. Fuse the interfacing to the wool according to the manufacturer's directions.

2. Fold the wool in half lengthwise with the interfacing on the inside. The fold is the bottom of the bag. Place one or two pins at the top and bottom.

3. Place the pumpkin piece on the wool, centered between the sides and approximately ¾" from the bottom fold. The wider border at the top accommodates the bottle cap and embellishments. Pin in place.

4. Gently pull up each side of the punched piece, one at a time, and apply glue to hold it in place. Let dry. Whipstitch around the punched piece with black sewing thread and remove the pins.

5. Fold the wool right sides together and double stitch a ¼" seam down each 7" side. Taper the top of each seam about 2" down, carefully cutting away the excess fabric. Turn the pouch inside out; place the side with the punched piece face down on a towel and steam press.

6. Insert the lining into the purse, wrong sides together. Fold down the tops of the pouch and lining to the inside. Pin in place, leaving a space for the cording at each side seam. There should be about 1¼" between the top of the punched design and the top of the purse. Insert about 2" of each end of the cording into the space at each seam between the lining and the outer part of the purse. Pin the cording, wool, and lining together. (It will be thick.)

7. Machine stitch the top edge of the purse, double stitching where the cording is inserted. Using six strands of floss and an embroidery needle, stitch in a primitive style around the top of the bag, just barely covering the machine stitching. Start with the light orange, then the magenta, and then the red.

8. Working on a scrap of wood with a hammer and nail, tap four holes in the bottle cap to resemble a four-hole button.

9. Stitch your bottle cap (without the punching) to the purse like a button. Use strong glue to attach the punched piece inside the bottle cap. Use your needle to push and poke the outer edge into the cap.

10. To make the beaded border around the edge of the pumpkin, string 10 or 12 assorted beads onto a beading needle. Stitch the beads along the edge. Add more beads to the needle and repeat until the border is finished. Finally, tack the beads down with sewing thread and a hand-sewing needle so they won't catch on anything.

Enchanting Dollhouse Rug

by Laurie Luke

Skill Level: Advanced • **Finished Size of Punching:** 4" x 6"

In the world of miniatures, teapots are no bigger than thimbles and teacups
are the size of peas—and this enchanting dollhouse rug fits right in!
Inspired by antique Oriental rugs, this heirloom-quality miniature
will be a cherished treasure for your dollhouse. This rug is
designed to achieve the miniature scale of 1" = 1'.

What You'll Need

1-strand punchneedle

Embroidery hoop or gripper frame

12" x 12" square of high-quality muslin

Fabric glue

Waxed paper or aluminum foil

Cotton Embroidery Floss *One skein of each unless otherwise noted.*		
Used For	**Color**	**DMC**
Outlining	Black	310 (2 skeins)
Flowers, fringe, border vines	Off-white	3774
Background	Blue	3808
Leaves, scrolls	Dark green	732
Leaves, scrolls	Light green	523
Scrolls, border	Dark pink	3858
Flowers, scrolls	Light pink	223

Punching

The pattern appears on page 73. Use one strand of floss for punching the rug and two strands for creating the fringe. To retain the fine details of this piece, set the gauge at about ¼".

1. With black, punch on all the lines of the design *except* for the flower centers and the vine border area. Leaving a space for the flower center, fill in the center medallion flower, the outer border, and the large, jagged black leaves. At this point your rug will look like one big black blob. Don't worry!

2. The vine border area is next. Punch the vines with a single row of off-white and fill in all the leaves with dark green. Outline around the vines, leaves, and flowers with black. With dark green, fill in all the remaining leaves of the design and the dots near the flowers. Outline all the edges of the larger leaves with light green. Punch the dots with light green too.

3. For the green scroll near the border, punch a single row of light green facing toward the center of the rug; then fill in the remaining green scroll with dark green. In the pink scroll area, punch a single outline row of light pink along the edge nearest the center of the rug; then fill in the rest of the scroll with dark pink. For the green scroll surrounding the center medallion, punch a single row of light green along the edge nearest the center of the rug. Fill in the remaining green scroll areas with dark green.

4. Now work the flowers. Outline each flower with a single row of off-white. Fill in each petal with either off-white or light pink, leaving a space for the flower center. Add a black center, punching only two or three loops.

5. With off-white, punch the flower stems, staying between the black lines. Fill in the vases, the off-white bands at the four arrow ends of the center medallion, and the centers of the two largest arrows. Punch a single row along the center vein of each large, jagged black leaf.

6. Now work the center medallion area. Within the off-white area, punch a single line of light pink around the edge next to the blue area. This will create a shadow. Fill in the remainder with off-white. Next, punch the four leaves surrounding the center flower using light green. For the background of the center medallion, punch a single row of dark pink to outline the flowers and leaves, and then fill in the rest of this background with light pink. Fill in the blue area of the medallion and the remaining blue area of the rug.

7. To work the off-white area near the border, begin by punching a shadow line of light pink next to the green scroll. Then fill in the remaining area with off-white. Do not shadow the pink scroll areas. Fill in the remaining area with off-white.

8. Make sure that all remaining small leaves and dots throughout the rug are filled with light green. Now fill in the rest of the area between the pink scrolls and the large jagged leaves with off-white.

9. Fill in the four off-white scrolls which appear at the midpoint of each side of the rug (these are the scrolls that touch the vine border).

10. To fill in the large pink areas and the pink area within the vine border, begin by punching a shadow line with dark pink all around these areas, including the flowers, leaves, vases, and so on. Fill in the remaining area with the light pink.

11. Now go back and add loops in any areas (flowers, the vine, stems, etc.) that may need to be more prominent.

12. For the fringe, set the gauge on your two- or three-strand needle to ⅞". Using two strands of off-white, punch a single row along both of the short ends of rug. You will have long punched loops. If the loops tangle, carefully work them back into place.

Finishing

1. Take the work off the hoop and trim the muslin to ¼". Cut slits every inch around the rug, being careful not to cut into your punching. Cut off the corners diagonally, leaving about ⅛" of muslin. Fold over and glue the ⅛" at one corner. Repeat for the remaining three corners. Fold over and glue the remaining edges, going 1" at a time and making sure you are folding enough of the muslin over to have a nice edge and square corners on the right side.

2. Spread the glue over the entire back of the rug, including the already-glued-down muslin edges. Press the back of the rug onto waxed paper or aluminum foil. Press the rug down to shape and block it and to remove any excess glue. Remove the rug from the waxed paper and let it dry, wrong side up.

3. To finish your rug, clip the loops of the fringe and straighten and trim the fringe to the desired length. Your rug is now ready to be put into your enchanted dollhouse!

Patterns and Templates

Kitty Pendant
Page 22

Memory Gift Jar
Page 26

← Stretch of the fabric →

Potted Pin
Page 24

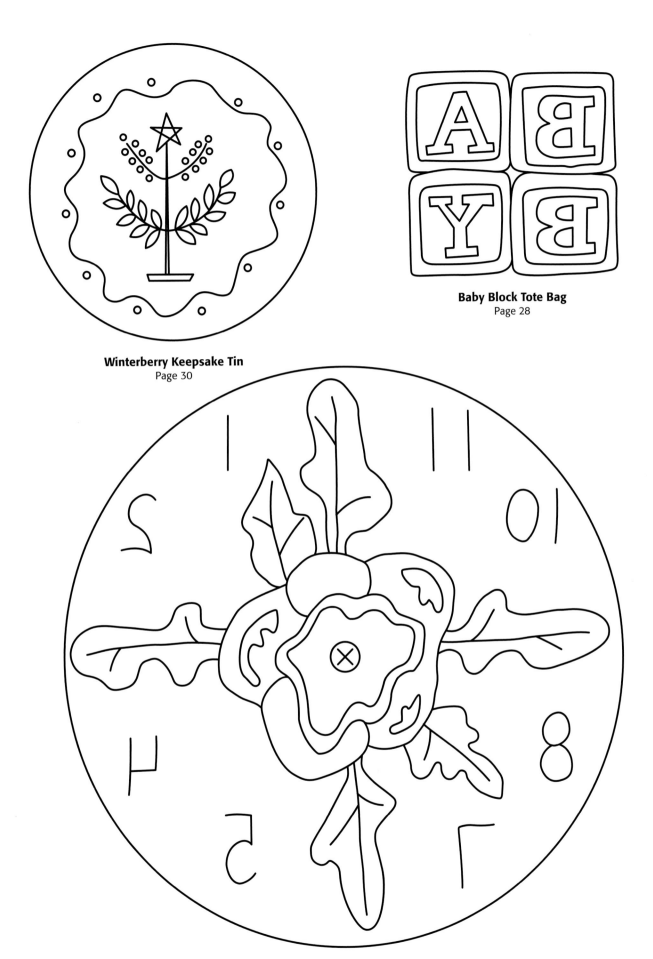

Winterberry Keepsake Tin
Page 30

Baby Block Tote Bag
Page 28

A Rose for Mommy Clock
Page 36

Two Rabbits Needle Case
Page 33

Snowman's Candy Jar
Page 42

Bird Blue Pillow
Page 38

Beach Crab Basket Topper
Page 44

Laura's Amaryllis Pillow
Page 47

Cut 1 from material for back of pouch.

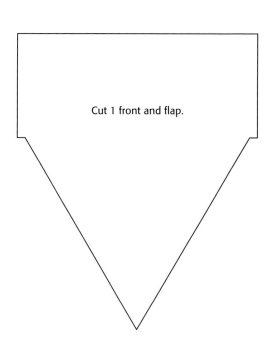

Cut 1 front and flap.

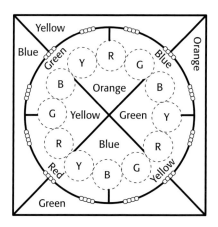

ⅎⅎⅎⅎ   4 seed beads

(R)   Mother-of-pearl button/
       color of buttonhole twist

Stitcher's Dream Pouch
Page 50

Raspberry Clusters Box
Page 53

Happy Jack Shoulder Purse
Page 59

October Bag
Page 56

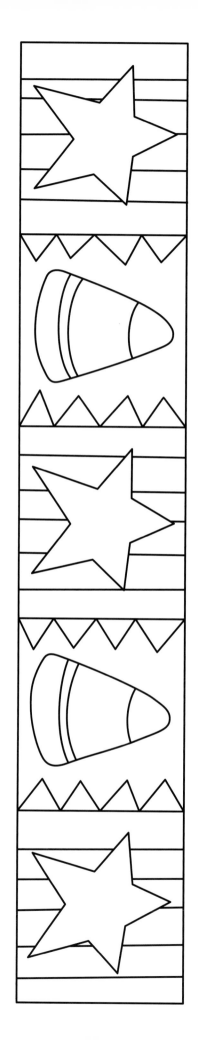

Enchanting Dollhouse Rug
Page 63

Resources

Punchneedle supplies can be found in needlework, craft, and quilt shops throughout the country, as well as online. Many of the designers in this book offer a wide array of supplies and materials as well as patterns. See "Designer Profiles" (page 76) for contact information. Manufacturers and distributors are listed below.

Punchneedles

Bernadine's Needle Art
1-888-884-8576
www.bernadinesneedleart.com
Bernadine's punchneedles

Birdhouse Enterprises
916-452-5212
www.gailbird.com
Igolochkoy punchneedles

CTR Needleworks
724-455-2111
www.ctrneedleworks.com
CTR punchneedles

Punch Needle Marketplace
1-800-272-1966
www.punchneedlemarketplace.com
Cameo Ultra Punch, Super Luxo punchneedles

Threads

Cotton Embroidery Floss—Solid Colors
Anchor
www.coatsandclark.com

DMC
www.dmc-usa.com

Finca by Presencia
www.presenciausa.com

Cotton Embroidery Floss—Overdyed Colors

The Gentle Art
www.thegentleart.com

Needle Necessities
www.needlenecessities.com

Weeks Dye Works
www.weeksdyeworks.com

Wool Thread

DMC Medicis
www.dmc-usa.com

Gloriana Lorikeet
www.glorianathreads.com

Needle Necessities French Wool Overdyed
www.needlenecessities.com

Renaissance Dyeing
www.renaissancedyeing.com

Other Threads

Soy Luster
877-592-6068
www.thepurepalette.com
Hand-dyed soy threads

Other Supplies

Lakeside Linens
360-428-8688
www.lakesidelinens.com
Hand-dyed weaver's cloth

Weeks Dye Works
919-772-9166
www.weeksdyeworks.com
Hand-dyed weaver's cloth

Woolen Whimsies
413-548-8040
www.woolenwhimsies.com
Gripper frames

Project-Specific Supplies

Kitty Pendant

Woolen Whimsies
413-548-8040
www.woolenwhimsies.com
Pendant frames

A Rose for Mommy Clock

Mad Hen Primitives
740-374-9722
www.madhen.com
Primitive wooden clock case

Beach Crab Basket Topper

Olde Colonial Designs
781-834-8836
www.oldecolonialdesigns.com
Nantucket candy basket

Wichelt Imports, Inc.
1-800-356-9516
www.wichelt.com
Mill Hill beads

Rainbow Gallery
www.rainbowgallery.com
Metallic braid

Stitcher's Dream Pouch
Tinsel Trading Company
www.tinseltrading.com
Antique metallic cord

Designer Profiles

By now, you are likely curious about the many talented individuals who designed the projects for this book. Here's your chance to find out a little more about each of them. Many of the designers, perhaps like you, discovered punchneedle after a lifetime of dabbling in a variety of needle arts, and so have brought with them years of experience in working with fiber. Once they began punching, the addiction took hold, and they added punchneedle designs to their professional offerings.

These designers graciously set aside time to create the patterns and projects that would pique your interest and show you a variety of methods for displaying your punched pieces. Be sure to explore their Web sites to discover the many other lovely works that they've created.

Tonya Benson

Tonya began sharing her artistic talents with the world more than 15 years ago when she and her parents sold handmade items at local craft shows. In 2001, Tonya and her parents fulfilled their dream by opening a shop in the historic town of Marietta, Ohio. The shop features a wide range of treasures, from hand-dyed wool and patterns to reproduction primitive furniture. Tonya has a particular knack for designing hooked rugs that reflect her love of the simplest things in life.

Web site: www.madhen.com
Email: madhen3@charterinternet.com

Pat Cross

Pat lives in Charlottesville, Virginia, with her husband, Tom, and three cats. She had been involved in counted cross-stitch, quilting, and other textile arts until she discovered rug hooking 15 years ago. Since then, she has been designing, teaching, and writing about rug hooking, and has gained national recognition as a designer and teacher. Pat enjoys translating her rug designs into miniature punchneedle pieces. Pat has published articles on a variety of topics relating to rug hooking and dyeing, and has written two books: *Purely Primitive: Hooked Rugs from Wool, Yarn, and Homespun Scraps* (Martingale & Company, 2003) and *Simply Primitive: Rug Hooking, Punchneedle, and Needle Felting* (Martingale & Company, 2006).

Email: Dye4Wool@aol.com
Phone: 434-244-5755

Charlotte Dudney

Charlotte Dudney is a nationally recognized punchneedle teacher and designs under the business name Designs from the Pep'r Pot. She fell in love with punchneedle because it reminded her of rug hooking in miniature. Charlotte lives in Arlington, Texas, with her husband, Fred. She travels extensively to teach and promote punchneedle. She was a featured teacher at the International Needleart Retailers Guild and the National NeedleArts Association for their 2005 markets. Charlotte holds virtual classes through her popular instructional DVD. Her Web site showcases her patterns and includes lots of useful information about common punchneedle problems and solutions, as well as some of the history of punchneedle.

Web site: www.russianpunchneedle.com
Email: thepeprpot@comcast.net
Phone: 817-633-6611

Lee Faulkner

Lee has been passionate about needlework since she was a child; she has done crewel, counted thread, primitive appliqué, rug hooking, and needlepoint. When a friend insisted on taking Lee to a display featuring Russian punchneedle, she discovered this form of needlework and immediately became addicted! Soon after, she began designing punchneedle patterns with the help of her sister, Laura, and miniaturizing the hooked rug designs of her friend Melissa Elliott. Lee teaches punchneedle and displays her work at folk-art shows. She loves helping others discover this wonderful needlework, and particularly savors the moment when someone realizes that something so tiny and perfect is also so simple and forgiving.

Web site: www.memescottage.com
Email: memescottagecollection@yahoo.com
Phone: 859-351-6164

Patricia Smith Gardner

Learning from her mother and grandmother, Patricia has been sewing and needle crafting as long as she can remember. She has tried nearly every form of craft and needlework, and loves to invent new ways of doing everything—with lots of trial and error. Professionally, Patricia is a designer of prototypes for the doll and soft toy industry, working with companies to develop products. She savors doing embroidery in her spare time. Patricia fell in love with the texture, density, and detail of punched pieces, and now focuses on working with one strand of cotton floss. She enjoys working with pieces in the folk-art tradition, with bright colors and a graphic border.

Email: pasg@comcast.net
Phone: 610-664-6970

Karen Amadio Gates

Karen has been creating needlework of one kind or another since childhood, and spent many years exploring various fiber-art forms—until she discovered punchneedle. Captivated by its resemblance to tiny hooked rugs, she is now well-known for her punched folk-art designs created with only a single strand of floss. Karen is a juried member of the Pennsylvania Guild of Craftsmen and has been recognized as one of the top 200 craftsmen in the country by *Early American Life* magazine. Her works have been featured in several magazines. She lives in historic Bucks County, Pennsylvania, with her husband, Tom, and sons, Tyler and Jordan.

Company name: Folk Art Designs
Web site: www.karengatesfolkart.com
Email: karen@karengatesfolkart.com
Phone: 215-766-0746

Brenda Gervais

Brenda was taught at a young age to be creative, imaginative, and to make do with what she had. This lesson flows over into her adult life. Since 1987, she has run a pattern and design business, Country Stitches. It was only recently that she discovered and fell in love with punchneedle and began creating designs under the name With Thy Needle and Thread. Brenda's eye for color and design has helped her create a variety of unique punchneedle patterns. Brenda feels very blessed to have the opportunity to do what she loves every day—create with her hands. She has two grown children, Erin and Matthew, and resides in Storm Lake, Iowa, with her husband, Dave.

Web site: www.countrystitchesonline.com
Email: order@countrystitchesonline.com
Phone: 712-732-5419

Sally Korte and Alice Strebel

Sally and Alice were brought together by a common love of primitive folk art. As these two young mothers created handcrafted gifts for craft sales, they found themselves continually appreciating each other's work and realized they were indeed kindred spirits. Before long, they joined together in business, publishing patterns and books featuring embellished clothing, primitive stitcheries, whimsical dolls, quilts, and other folk-art pieces designed with a charmingly naive look. Their shop, Kindred Spirits, offers a wide range of clothing, patterns, books, and supplies for a variety of fiber arts, and hosts Kindred Spirits Retreats. Sally and Alice lecture and teach internationally and give motivational speeches on personal creativity.

Web site: www.kindredspiritsdesigns.com
Email: kspirits@voyager.net
Phone: 937-435-7758

Laurie Luke

Many think of a dollhouse as a little girl's toy, but collecting miniatures is also a very grown-up hobby. As a child, Laurie loved dollhouses, and as an adult is still intrigued and inspired by antique dollhouses. Discovering punchneedle was a dream come true because it allowed Laurie to miniaturize antique Oriental rugs. With floss as her palette, she has been designing and creating miniature rugs and needlework for over 25 years. Hoping to offer patterns soon, she sells finished rugs on eBay, and also creates commissioned pieces. She admits that it's sometimes hard letting go of the finished pieces, but knowing that her rugs are in incredible dollhouses all over the country brings her pure joy!

Email: foofy@gwtc.net
Phone: 605-286-3814
eBay seller ID: foofy1

Penny McAllister

Fiber, fabric, beads, and color have always fascinated Penny. Growing up with grandmothers who were always busy with their hands, Penny developed an artistic flair at an early age. As an elementary school librarian, she was surrounded by the primary colors of construction paper, tempera paint, and children's art. After leaving the working world behind, Penny became an accomplished folk artist working in papier-mâché. When she saw punchneedle for the first time, she was captivated by the small details it could achieve, and by its resemblance to rug hooking. Before long, she was transforming her papier-mâché designs into punchneedle works, thus creating a new dimension to her artistry.

Web site: www.pennymcallister.com
Email: penny@pennymcallister.com

Cherie Ralston

Cherie was introduced to miniature punchneedle embroidery by Ellen Grau, who gave her a 10-minute lesson while standing in the aisle at a trade show. From that moment on, Cherie was hooked! Cherie is an accomplished quilt designer whose patterns are sought out by fiber artists throughout the country. She has collaborated with well-known quilt artists Gerry Kimmel-Carr, Karla Menaugh, Barbara Brackman, Alma Allen, and Jan Patek. Cherie teaches quilting and punchneedle to fiber artists.

Email: cherieralston@sunflower.com

Margaret Shaw

In her early years, Margaret explored many textile mediums, such as weaving, spinning, knitting, quilting, wool appliqué, and rug hooking. She was inspired by early American crafts. She later began to employ paint, and her yearning to recycle led her to paint folk art on found or salvaged materials. Her personal interest in protecting the earth is reflected in the renewable resources she uncovers and works with. Today, Margaret paints on salvage, and also designs punchneedle and rug-hooking patterns that are based on her original painted folk art.

Web sites: www.PunchNeedlePatterns.com, www.MShawFolkArt.com, and www.ArtPatternDesigns.com
Email: margshaw@worldnet.att.net
Phone: 734-428-8497

Missy Stevens

A professional weaver and an embroidery enthusiast, Missy discovered punchneedle and was entranced by its potential to "paint" with thread. Missy includes nature, textiles, animals, color, dreams, and mystical symbols into her artwork—all things that she loves. As each layer of stitching enriches the final piece, so each layer of a design deepens the impact of the finished piece. Missy sells her one-of-a-kind thread paintings through art galleries and occasionally teaches classes.

Web site: www.missystevens.com
Email: missy@missystevens.com

Linda Stolz

The designer and owner of Erica Michaels Designs, Linda has been an avid needleworker and seam-stress for over 30 years. She grew up exposed to embroidery, quilting, crocheting, knitting, and counted cross-stitch. She began designing cross-stitch pieces, and was instantly hooked when she saw punchneedle work for the first time. She learned quickly and became one of the first designers in the counted-thread industry to add punchneedle to her line of designs. She teaches punchneedle and needlework around the country at retail shops, industry trade shows, and needlework retreat weekends. Linda is married with one son, named Eric Michael—she uses a feminine version of her son's name for her design studio.

Web site: www.ericamichaels.com
Email: emstitch@charter.net

Shawn Williams

Shawn can't remember a time when she didn't have some type of craft project underway, mostly needlework. Her mother seemed to know everything about needlework, and shared her knowledge and love of textiles with Shawn. Shawn thought she'd seen every type of needlework possible, and yet punchneedle was new to her. As an adult, Shawn formed her own pattern company. At first, her designs focused on cloth doll patterns; then embroidery, wool appliqué, and penny rugs—and now punchneedle embroidery. Shawn was particularly delighted to be able to teach her mom something new in the world of needlework, and now her mom loves punchneedle too!

Company name: Threads That Bind
Web site: www.threadsthatbindonline.com
Email: shawn@threadsthatbindonline.com

About the Editor

Linda Repasky

Like so many punchers, Linda Repasky has enjoyed dabbling in a wide variety of fiber arts over the years. A long-time rug hooker, she discovered the joys of punchneedle several years ago and has been punching ever since. For the past two years, she has been honored to have been selected as one of the country's top 200 craftsmen by *Early American Life* magazine for her punchneedle creations. She travels throughout the country teaching punchneedle skills to a variety of fiber enthusiasts. She is also the author of *Miniature Punchneedle Embroidery* (Martingale and Company, 2006), which provides comprehensive instructions on punching. She lives in rural western Massachusetts, where she creates punchneedle designs and makes gripper frames.

Web site: www.woolenwhimsies.com
Email: Linda@woolenwhimsies.com

New and Bestselling Titles from

America's Best-Loved Craft & Hobby Books®
America's Best-Loved Knitting Books®

America's Best-Loved Quilt Books®

NEW RELEASES
Adoration Quilts
Better by the Dozen
Blessed Home Quilt, The
Hooked on Wool
It's a Wrap
Let's Quilt!
Origami Quilts
Over Easy
Primitive Gatherings
Quilt Revival
Sew One and You're Done
Scraps of Time
Simple Chenille Quilts
Simple Traditions
Simply Primitive
Surprisingly Simple Quilts
Two-Block Theme Quilts
Wheel of Mystery Quilts

APPLIQUÉ
Appliqué Takes Wing
Easy Appliqué Samplers
Garden Party
Raise the Roof
Stitch and Split Appliqué
Tea in the Garden

LEARNING TO QUILT
Happy Endings, Revised Edition
Loving Stitches, Revised Edition
Magic of Quiltmaking, The
Quilter's Quick Reference Guide, The
Your First Quilt Book (or it should be!)

PAPER PIECING
40 Bright and Bold Paper-Pieced Blocks
50 Fabulous Paper-Pieced Stars
300 Paper-Pieced Quilt Blocks
Easy Machine Paper Piecing
Quilt Block Bonanza
Quilter's Ark, A
Show Me How to Paper Piece

PIECING
40 Fabulous Quick-Cut Quilts
101 Fabulous Rotary-Cut Quilts
365 Quilt Blocks a Year: Perpetual
    Calendar
1000 Great Quilt Blocks
Big 'n Easy
Clever Quilts Encore
Once More around the Block
Stack a New Deck

QUILTS FOR BABIES & CHILDREN
American Doll Quilts
Even More Quilts for Baby
More Quilts for Baby
Quilts for Baby
Sweet and Simple Baby Quilts

SCRAP QUILTS
More Nickel Quilts
Nickel Quilts
Save the Scraps
Successful Scrap Quilts
    from Simple Rectangles
Treasury of Scrap Quilts, A

TOPICS IN QUILTMAKING
Alphabet Soup
Cottage-Style Quilts
Creating Your Perfect Quilting Space
Focus on Florals
Follow the Dots . . . to Dazzling Quilts
More Biblical Quilt Blocks
Scatter Garden Quilts
Sensational Sashiko
Warm Up to Wool

CRAFTS
Bag Boutique
Purely Primitive
Scrapbooking Off the Page…and on the
    Wall
Stamp in Color
Vintage Workshop, The: Gifts for All
    Occasions

KNITTING & CROCHET
200 Knitted Blocks
365 Knitting Stitches a Year: Perpetual
    Calendar
Crochet from the Heart
First Crochet
First Knits
Fun and Funky Crochet
Handknit Style
Knits from the Heart
Little Box of Knitted Ponchos and Wraps,
    The
Little Box of Knitted Throws, The
Little Box of Crocheted Hats and Scarves,
    The
Little Box of Scarves, The
Little Box of Scarves II, The
Little Box of Sweaters, The
Pursenalities
Sensational Knitted Socks

Our books are available at bookstores and your favorite craft,
fabric, and yarn retailers. If you don't see the title
you're looking for, visit us at
www.martingale-pub.com
or contact us at:

1-800-426-3126

International: 1-425-483-3313 **Fax:** 1-425-486-7596
Email: info@martingale-pub.com